THE CORROSION OF THE SELF
Society's Effects on People

The publication of this work has been aided by a grant from the Andrew W. Mellon Foundation

THE CORROSION
OF THE SELF

Society's Effects on People

THOMAS KREILKAMP

New York · New York University Press · 1976

Library of Congress Catalog Card Number: 75-13520

ISBN: 0-8147-4561-X

Library of Congress Cataloging in Publication Data

Kreilkamp, Thomas A   1941-
  The corrosion of the self.

  Bibliography: p.
  1. Social psychology. 2. Social institutions.
3. Self. I. Title.
HM251.K635   301.1   75-13520
ISBN 0-8147-4561-X

MANUFACTURED IN THE UNITED STATES OF AMERICA

For Vera

Foreword

This book was written while I was teaching at the University of Massachusetts at Boston; the energy behind it derives from my teaching and the intellectual stimulation of my students there. Special thanks are due to Henry Murray, Joe de Rivera, and Isidor Chein, who provided me with models of what psychological thinking might resemble, and to Bernie Kramer, who prodded me to actually write the book.

A summer faculty growth grant from the University of Massachusetts in 1970, and a summer grant from the National Endowment for the Humanities in 1974 helped me do some of the work on this book.

Many people read an early version of the book and offered helpful comments: Lois Biener, Sheldon Cashdan, Isidor Chein, Lajos Heder, Jane Keddy, Joel Kovel, Sadie Kreilkamp, David McClelland, Elliot Mishler, Don Mixon, Tom Pettigrew, Everett Wilson, and Gordon Zahn. If I have not benefited from their comments, the responsibility is mine.

Contents

Introduction

The primary aim of this book is to provide a conceptual framework within which certain general issues can be considered. One such issue is the relation of the self to the society it lives in. The need for such a conceptual framework may not be evident. After all, most of us manage to comprehend as much of our complicated web of relationships as we need to. We each have some grasp of how we fit into our society and think we know when we feel constrained and when free.

But this dimension of constraint and freedom is exactly what needs analysis, for it dominates much contemporary thought about the self and society. For example, we conventionally think, these days, in terms of conformity. The self conforms to social pressures, we say. The latent image here is of a self, separate and free, which yields to some outside pressure. Does this image make any sense? That is one of the questions which this book will consider.

The image of people existing in chains and struggling to be free is a powerful one, and it underlies much contemporary criticism of our society. Contemporary social commentary often takes the form of critical and heated objection to the way things are in American society. These criticisms range from specific analyses of the harm done by specific social institutions (the school, the family, the mental hospital) to wholesale indictments of our entire society. Do these criticisms make sense?

There is no easy way to answer such a question, and no clear-cut answer will be presented here. But I shall try to show how the most interesting contemporary social theory bears on these criticisms. The conceptual issue is: To what extent is the image of people oppressed by social institutions reasonable to social psychologists, given their present theoretical grasp and understanding?

A secondary aim of this book is to inform the reader about the conceptual side of contemporary social psychology. People do not seem to appreciate the theoretical understanding of self-and-society relations which contemporary social psychology has to offer—at least judging by public debate on such issues as the family and school and their effects on the formation of self. It is true that psychology is very popular, as the success of the magazine *Psychology Today* attests; nonetheless, social psychology generally permeates public understanding only when one or another of its experiments becomes famous (or notorious, as the case may be). For example, many people know about the Milgram experiments at Yale: that most of his subjects agreed to give shocks to someone they had just met simply because they were asked to do so. But social psychology does not consist simply of several ingenious provocative experiments. Latent in social psychology and not generally appreciated is a powerful theoretical grasp of some of the complicated relationship between self and society. The secondary aim of this book, then, is to make available to the general reader some knowledge of this theoretic side of social psychology.

Radical criticisms of our society became widespread during the late sixties. To show to what extent the sweeping criticisms make sense, I shall analyze one particular critical stance: a description of our high schools and the schooling process in general in America. However, this is simply to provide a reference point; the focus in this book is not on the criticisms themselves, but on the intelligibility and scope of the ideas about man and society expressed by the theorists we will discuss. Do the ideas of these writers help us to understand the nature of the relationship between each of us and the society we live in? Are their ideas pertinent and useful in the debate about our schools?

Contemporary social psychology is largely experimental, but the theorists to be discussed here are not experimental; in fact, they are not generally known as social psychologists. Nonetheless they speak to the central issues of social psychology more pertinently than does most of the experimental literature. Thus the third aim of this book is to articulate a view of what social psychology might become: something more than a collection of experiments. Important as experiments are for the development of a science, some broad theory is also needed. Discovering which aspects of contemporary social theory seem to apply to social psychological problems is important for the development of social psychology. As I consider Thomas Schelling, Erving Goffman, Ronald Laing, Herbert Marcuse, and Kenneth Burke, the reader may be persuaded that these authors have an important contribution to make.

Why these particular writers? First and most important, they are fascinating and original. Second, their ideas for the most part have not been integrated into the main body of social psychology; except for Erving Goffman, who is very familiar, these men are not well known to social psychologists. Laing, of course, and Marcuse, as well, are familiar names, but their ideas have not had much impact on the thinking of social psychologists, perhaps because the implications of their ideas for social psychology have not been understood. Schelling and Burke are probably relatively unfamiliar names; the first is an economist, the second a literary critic. But each has postulated ways of looking at social and psychological questions which deserve some attention. These writers are also important because their views fit together in a way not presently well understood. My focus is partly integrative here: to show how writers of diverse backgrounds and intentions contribute to a view of man and society which will be genuinely useful in understanding specific social problems.

One problem with these theoretical approaches is that

often they lack supporting evidence; or worse, they leave unclear the whole question of how one would gather evidence either for or against them. Often they are tangential to issues of evidence. However, they are not tangential to certain realms of social reality, as will be made clear. There ought to be some benefit in bringing together here a respect for experimentation with a respect for theory. So often the people who generate the one have contempt for the other. It is difficult to see how a genuine science of social psychology can develop out of such a situation.

Thus, this book is directed at students or any general readers who want to develop an understanding of society and its relation to the self; who want to begin a study of social psychology with some general account of the kinds of problems which social psychology attempts ultimately to elucidate. But the book is also directed at the general reader who is familiar with any one of the writers being considered, who wants to get some idea of how what one writer says fits into what other writers are saying, and how all their ideas bear on matters of general social controversy. Finally, of course, the book has something to say to professionals in the field of social psychology; for this book attempts to articulate a conceptual framework which will make clearer how social psychology can be broadened theoretically, and how it can be brought to bear on matters of deep social importance. For social psychology needs theories as well as finely wrought experiments, and social psychology has from its beginnings been in search of social relevance.

Chapter 1 considers contemporary social psychology. The first aspect of social psychology that draws our attention is the lack of any unifying theory to unite sociology and psychology in the way that the very existence of the discipline has always promised to provide someday. This point will be illustrated by an analysis of one attempt to forge a truly social-psychological understanding of a given phenomenon—that of alienation, as revealed in Kenneth Keniston's book, *The Uncommitted*. Second, the extent to which contemporary social psychology bears directly on social problems will be evaluated by an examination of two books which argue that it does have social relevance. One of these books is a recent social psychology text book by a well-known experimental social psychologist, Elliot Aronson's *The Social Animal.* The second book is the familiar *Walden II* by B. F. Skinner.

The underlying point in the first chapter is that without an adequate broad-gauge theory, one which can unify social psychology at least to some extent, one which can tie together the disparate empirical and theoretical analyses which are already present, social psychologists will continue to have difficulty in persuasively analyzing contemporary social problems. Their analyses will continue to have an *ad hoc* character; they will continue to be worked out separately for each social problem, following the model which is dominant presently, namely the model which says that if there is a social problem, then social soctientists should be hired to solve or help us solve it. So each problem area has its research grants and its investigators, but this apparatus leads too exclusively to an empirical approach not held together by any coherent theory. Each investigator gathers data about his problem area and then presents them within whatever framework comes easiest to hand. This approach will never, even ultimately, illuminate social problems in a way that might lead to the formation of consistent public policy or public understanding.

The second chapter deals with an example of contemporary social criticism, to see what ideas underlie it and to try to see what crucial issues are contained within it, to which social psychology might plausibly be supposed to have something to contribute. This critical analysis of our high schools I take as representative of other critical analyses of other social institutions. Most of these contemporary social criticisms seem to have various points in common: for example, they all posit the individual as oppressed by a social institution. This concept of oppression will be discussed at some length.

Succeeding chapters consider various contemporary social theorists: Ronald Laing, Erving Goffman, Carl Rogers,

Thomas Schelling, and Kenneth Burke. I shall try to lay bare some (but not all) of the fundamental outlines of their thought; and to evaluate their ideas for internal consistency, for their bearing on the critical issues raised earlier in discussing the analysis of our high schools, and in light of the ideas of each preceding writer as we continue.

Finally, the concluding chapter will tie the preceding analyses of these various writers together, showing how they each contribute in important and overlapping ways to our understanding of the relation between man and society; the very relation which social psychology is intended to illuminate and the very relation which social criticism purports to understand. This concluding chapter will review the most significant of the ideas which have emerged in the preceding discussions.

CHAPTER 1

Contemporary Social Psychology

Some best-selling books are about what social psychologists would call interpersonal processes (Eric Berne's *Games People Play* of a few years ago, and *I'm OK, You're OK*, by Thomas Harris). Encounter groups (and all the other groups) are a popular phenomenon which seems sometimes to approach the proportions of a mania. Interpersonal processes and all group phenomena are part of what is usually called social psychology, that part of psychology or sociology lying uneasily on the borders between those two amorphous disciplines which attempts to study relations among people and the ways in which those relations influence and are influenced by the people engaging in them. Not everyone reads the books that are known within the social sciences as social psychology books, but Americans seem fascinated by the kinds of issues that absorb the energies of social psychologists. Why do individuals sometimes give in to group pressures (the problem of conformity); why do individuals sometimes not give in to the conventional pressures (the problem of deviance in all its varied manifestations); to what extent do group pressures warp true human being; is the family a well-designed group for raising children and satisfying people? These questions are very important to contemporary Americans if one can judge by conversation and magazine and newspaper articles. And these questions are the sort that social psychologists try to grapple with, which serve as conceptual focal points for the development of their discipline.

What makes social psychology interesting is its tentative promise—contained in its very name—to say something about the social constituents of personality, or about the psychological nature of sociality. How and where do society and individual people interpenetrate? Social psychology sounds as though it ought to have some kind of reply to that sort of question; and contemporary concerns such as conformity, alienation, integration, the nuclear family and concomitant sexual roles, all the civil libertarian issues which arise when the rights of the individual seem to stand opposed to the rights of the society; these and many other problems seem to rest squarely within the boundaries of social psychology. Thus, insofar as social psychology addresses itself to these questions, it is bound to seem interesting; it promises to provide some connections.

In order to understand why social psychology sometimes seems not to fulfill that promise, one must understand that it is divided—as is so much of psychology—between the experimenters and the others. The experimenters think experimentation is primary, and that if an issue does not lend itself to experiments, it should have less claim on our scarce resources of time and energy. The others think instead that the primary criterion for deciding to study something is its importance, appeal, interest, relevance; once having chosen a topic for study, they use whatever means seem available; if not experimental, other kinds. Experimentalists dominate social psychology; however, this other point of view, although it is more common outside the profession than in it, is taken by some accepted professionals. And it is this latter attitude—that taking certain theoretical problems seriously is as important as doing acceptable experiments—that informs this book. These fundamental problems of social psychology are, for example, to know precisely how individuals depend on society for sustenance; precisely how they are capable of taking stances in opposition to social pressures; what the processes are which build up connections between individuals, and yet somehow lay the groundwork for severing those connections.

Many critics of the experimental part of social psychology see it as retreating from confronting general social problems such as these. But it is too harsh to say that all of social psychology is narrow and irrelevant to larger social issues. In fact, many social psychologists are deeply concerned with them. Through some studies which, although nonexperimental, attempt some degree of rigor, a trail leading toward the larger and fundamental questions lying at the roots of social psychology is being hewn. These questions need some kind of rough, yet pertinent, answers if social psychology is to attain any conceptual breadth.

INTEGRATING PSYCHOLOGY AND SOCIOLOGY

Kenneth Keniston's *The Uncomitted* takes up the basic concerns we have been discussing. Keniston had the larger questions in view while carrying out his study of alienation in young men at Harvard in the late fifties and early sixties. In his book, he does not simply show us some alienated young men; he seeks a true integration of sociology and psychology, to forge a true social psychology which will not simply be a pastiche. His problems in doing what he set out to do are instructive; they illustrate a very real conceptual difficulty, not so much Keniston's as it is that of social psychology.[1] For in a sense we are still seeking a coherent social psychology, although we have many fine psychologists and sociologists hard at work. Something vital is missing, and it is not so much a lack of resources for studies, not a lack of appreciation of scientific methodology, or a shortage of talented people, but rather a neglect of the unifying power of what theoretical gains have been won.

Keniston's attempt and his failure are valuable in that they illuminate the problem posed by the very existence of

1. John Seeley makes much the same point at many places in his collection of essays, *The Americanization of the Unconscious*. See particularly the "Epilogue," pp. 449-52.

social psychology. The field has grown out of psychology and sociology and does not yet really have a viewpoint of its own. Social psychology is still made up of psychologists, trained in graduate programs of psychology, who are interested in society enough to infuse their writing and thinking with a social perspective; and sociologists, trained in graduate schools of sociology, who are interested enough in the psyche to infuse their writings and thinking with a psychological orientation. There is as yet no real merging of the two disciplines, even in places where they both form one academic department. This is so not simply because professionals who are trained in one kind of graduate program (either psychology or sociology) become incapable of attaining a wider point of view. Having a Ph.D. program in social psychology which is independent of either department would not help because the root of the problem is not in the graduate training. The problem is that no conceptual framework exists to integrate the two disciplines (at least, none that satisfies very many). The fundamental concepts which would show what is happening at the juncture of sociology and psychology—concepts which, if they existed, would in fact create the field of social psychology—are lacking. The field exists because it seems reasonable enough that there should be some overlap between what is called sociology and what is called psychology. But although some of us call ourselves social psychologists (by virtue of our training, or of our jobs, or of our interests), we still lack a conceptual structure which would, in a convincing fashion, forge a coherent social science out of what is now a disparate group of people doing disparate kinds of research.

THE UNCOMMITTED

Keniston makes clear at the beginning of his book that he thinks alienation is an issue of growing concern for Americans:

Increasingly, the vocabulary of social commentary is dominated by terms that characterize the sense of

growing distance between men and their former objects of affection. Alienation, estrangement, disaffec-
tion, anomie, withdrawal, disengagement, separation,
non-involvement, apathy, indifference, and neutral-
ism—all of these terms point to a sense of loss, a growing gap between men and their social world. The drift
of our time is away from connection, relation, com-
munion and dialogue, and our intellectual concerns
reflect this conviction. (p. 1) [2]

He wants to study the general question of why this growing
sense of alienation characterizes contemporary American
life. He points out that "there are two major traditions in
studying a process like alienation" (p. 6). One is the psychological tradition: seeing alienation as an individual
problem, tracking down individuals who have this problem,
and trying to figure out why they have it. The second tradition might be called sociological: seeing alienation as a
social process involving a response to stresses and strains in
the structure of social life. He then makes clear his ambition
to connect and combine these two traditions. Yet, as he
himself says, "merely to hyphenate these two traditions is
not enough: 'psycho-social' or 'socio-psychological' approaches also require new ways of thinking, new concepts,
new understandings of how men and society connect . . . "
(p. 7).

Keniston has accurately characterized the problem which
concerns us here: contemporary social psychology seems to
have no conceptual structure which would adequately
reflect its novel point of view. The point of the following
analysis of his book is to make clear the kinds of problems
encountered in doing what he tries to do. We simply lack
the kind of conceptual structure which would adequately
link social and psychological modes of explanation. Keniston's book is a valuable illustration of how even a researcher
who is aware of the problem and who is trying explicitly to

2. The page references are to the 1970 Dell paperback edition of
Keniston's *The Uncommitted*.

make a connection between psychological and sociological modes of explanation and thinking can fail.

The first indication that Keniston has not fulfilled his high ambitions of integrating psychological and sociological modes of thinking comes in the table of contents, which makes clear that the book is divided in half. The first half is called "Alienated Youth" and the second half "Alienating Society." Thus, from the very beginning he makes clear that his analysis of alienation will separate the psychological from the sociological. Or, at least, this is what the table of contents implies; but is this in fact the case?

In the first half of his book, Keniston discusses twelve male undergraduates whom he studied intensively (along with others) in an effort to comprehend their alienation. These twelve males scored very high on the various indices of alienation Keniston had developed. How are these young men studied? In ways traditional to clinical psychology. They were interviewed at some length; they were given various projective tests and asked about their lives, their dreams, their fears. Much is made of the analysis of their Thematic Apperception Test (TAT) stories, and the TAT, of course, is a well-known projective test, whose construction and interpretation rely heavily on psychoanalytic ideas about personality structure and functioning. The methodology of the study was restricted almost totally to asking these young men about themselves in a variety of ways. (Although Keniston alludes to other more observational and experimental studies that were carried out on his subject sample, it is not clear that he used these other data in his study; and if he used them, it is not clear exactly how.) This is, of course, the clinical method par excellence, as developed by Freud and others since. What this method leads to is an interpretation of alienation, as expressed by these twelve young men, which relies heavily on Freudian concepts and a very Freudian picture of how family background and interaction (as assessed not through observation, but through the dreams, memories, and TAT stories of the subjects who are eighteen to twenty years old at the time) produce various kinds of personality constellations.

Essentially we get a case history of the sort a psychiatrist might write after seeing a patient in therapy for a year or so. And, in fact, the first half of the book begins with a case history of one representative alienated student.

Clearly, the conceptual structure of the first half of the book—of the research upon which the book is based—is largely psychoanalytic. The psychoanalytic influence is seen in the methods used to carry out the study: studying a small number of subjects and relying heavily on projective tests and interviews for material. The psychoanalytic influence is also seen in the analysis made of the material these methods provided: the analysis is permeated by the vocabulary of psychoanalytic theory; and the crucial components of the analysis—the Oedipal relations between the child and his parents—are clearly psychoanalytic.

These comments point out the obvious to some extent; certainly Keniston would not dispute this analysis of the first half of the book. What is of great interest is the extent to which his explanation of alienation, in the first half of the book, if persuasive, cuts the ground from under his interest in showing how alienation in America has larger social sources. The methodology he has chosen and the data he presents show that alienation arises from certain kinds of family situations; and the conclusion seems to be that alienation is what you get when you have a particular type of mother and father together with a particular type of child. Keniston does hint that there are features of American life which make this kind of pattern—the co-presence of this type of mother, father, and child—very prevalent; but nowhere does he expand on this, nor does he offer any data relevant to this point. This would, of course, be an interesting point to try to document as a way of providing social context for the data in the first half of the book.

DATA

The issue of data is crucial to a comprehension of the general effect of any social psychology book. All the data in Keniston's are concentrated in the first half of the book; that is, they are psychological data, and are analyzed from a psychoanalytic point of view. When he turns—abruptly—to a consideration of the broader social roots of alienation in American life, his transition is not very compelling; he provides no evidence of any need for a perspective any broader than that offered in the first half of the book. The second half of the book is discontinuous with the first half; it seems to have no connection with it, greatly weakening his argument that to account for and understand alienation we need some combination of psychological and sociological perspectives.

In the second half of the book, Keniston discusses in very general terms various general criticisms and theories about the state of present-day American society (those of Paul Goodman, Edgar Friedenberg, David Riesman, Erik Erikson, etc.). There is an attempt made to link these different ideas together, but virtually no attempt—certainly no sustained systematic attempt—to link these discussions with the earlier half of the book. It is almost as though this second half of the book were conceived and written independently of the first, then published together with it because of some overlapping themes and concerns.

HOW TO IMPROVE KENISTON'S ANALYSIS

Keniston might have made the second half seem more connected with the first by more clearly showing how the various themes discussed in the second half are woven into the fabric of the lives of the young men he had analyzed in the first half. He suggests how he might have done this, as when he says that "possessive mothers may be made more possessive by the limitations of their husband's jobs . . ." (p. 7). His possessive mothers, who have played a role in the development of alienation in their sons, may perhaps in turn be a reflection of the situations in which they find themselves in contemporary America: the nuclear family where the man is often out of the house, working on an activity whose pertinence to the life of the woman and the household is often purely financial; the woman who does not work, whose husband's work takes him away and is not interesting to her to boot.

If Keniston had explored this theme, he might have made viable connections between the two halves of his book. An even better method would have been to write the book so that the sociological and psychological parts interpenetrated. But this could not happen in any legitimate and natural sense unless the methodology of the study were altered so as to take into account both the need for psychological data from the individuals involved and the need for a more sociological kind of data about the situations in which they found themselves. It is here that my suggestions become labored, since any kind of adequate suggestions would depend upon a prior conception about what kinds of data connections are worth looking for; one cannot look for data without some general conception, without some sense of what questions are worth asking. It is this general sense that is difficult—but not impossible—to arrive at.

For example, Keniston does say some interesting things which would neatly fit into the kind of framework he seems to be striving to attain. For example, he gives a sensible account of how alienation in these young men receives a fair measure of social support. As he points out, thoroughgoing alienation would be difficult to sustain in a social context where there was no support for such a posture (p. 71). This is an important point since it works against the naïve view that alienation is a consequence of only certain bad parts of our social system, the sort of view that proceeds from a naïve functionalism which sees lamentable traits in human beings (greed, jealousy, and, in this case, alienation) as arising from some kind of failure of our social structure, some kind of unfortunate arrangement of social forces. The naïveté lies in assuming that any human trait has only one simple set of causes. As Keniston makes clear at the beginning of his book (pp. 7 ff.), most things of interest to social scientists have many causes which interact in a very complicated manner. Alienation as a constellation of attitudes needs not only an emotionally receptive base created through a history of upbringing in a nuclear family dominated by a possessive mother and a rather withdrawn father (etc.); but, to take root, it needs further support on a broader cultural level (for example, the student finds writers who espouse views similar to those slowly emerging in his own mind). If we pursue this matter, we can see how alienation can be traced to its familial roots: we see the mother and father conspiring unintentionally to create a son who has a distrust of appearances, one of the many attitudes which form part of what Keniston calls the alienation syndrome. But we also see how alienation can be traced to its cultural roots: we all live in a culture where distrust of appearances is highly valued in certain spheres, for example, in the sciences. As Keniston cogently remarks:

> . . . distrust of appearances is not only a cardinal tenet of much depth psychology (which alerts us to the unfathomed impulses beneath our civilized rationalizations), but of Marxism (which shows class interest lurking beneath most statements about society). . . . (p. 71)

Both depth psychology (psychoanalytic views) and Marxism aspire to be scientific, and both partake of this distrust of appearances. Thus Keniston has some acute ideas of where to look, in seeking connections between psychological and sociological issues; but the data he has collected are rather unremittingly psychological, weakening his argument about the complexity of the roots of alienation.

The key to seeing the extent to which Keniston's thought is fundamentally psychological rather than truly social-psychological is in the way in which he takes so for granted that alienation is a problem or a sign of something being wrong whose field of expression (as it were) is the individual.[3] This is surely an orthodox psychological point of view. There are other ways to posit alienation, which might have led in other directions when it came to preparing a study. But his

3. I should make clear that this is not what Keniston says; this is my interpretation of his study. The way he defines the data field of relevance is what leads me to this interpretation.

way of conceiving of alienation—as a problem manifesting itself in these young men—leads him to study the roots of the problem in the way known so well now to psychologists: projective testing, exploring early memories, looking for unconscious ambivalences and conflicts, and the like.

Had Keniston begun thinking of alienation (from society, from socially defined goals, ambitions, etc.) as a healthy response by an individual to a distorted social situation, he might instead have begun looking—when it came time to collect data—at the strains in society, at the conflicts within our social structure, and then tried to show how these in turn give rise to alienation on the individual level. As an example of what is meant by considering alienation as a healthy response, look at the thinking that points out how an individual, in order to become distinct from his parents, has to push off from them (stand in opposition to them, be contrary, be negative); or the kind of thinking, in a different tradition, that talks about the individual necessity of taking a stand against reality, showing how one stands apart from the surrounding reality (by existentially making decisions which define that reality anew, which transform that reality). In both these views, alienation—as a separation from one's surroundings—would be vital to growth. One could argue that alienation exists in all younger people (under age twenty, let us say) insofar as they are healthy, and then is sustained (in young adults aged eighteen to twenty) in societies where the social structures are so stressful and nonfulfilling as to make living within them seem pointless. Keniston shares some of this mode of thinking, but his methodology does not allow him to do full justice to it.

In fact, what is paradoxical about Keniston's book is that he wants to argue—in the introduction for example—that it is, in fact, *societal* pressures which play the dominant role in creating the alienation of these talented young men. Here he thinks that the field of expression of alienation (the place where one looks to find manifestations of alienation, the level at which one tries to collect data concerning alienation) is the individual, but he seems to think that the primary (not the only) causes (supports, forces, pressures) of that alienation are social in nature. But the data he chooses to collect do not enable him to make this line of argument compelling.

This analysis of Keniston's book tries to make clear that its methodology and conceptual power derive mostly from psychology (specifically, those parts of psychology which are clinical), and that this approach is inadequate to his purpose as he himself defines it. In order to provide some clarity, we have tried to differentiate the field of expression of a given phenomenon such as alienation from the structural and dynamic forces which operate in that field (the causes as we would ordinarily refer to them). We can see the field in which alienation is expressed as the individual; this is what Keniston does. Or we could see the field as the society; if we had this latter view, the domain from which we derive our data would be different from the one Keniston relies on, and our methods would probably (although not necessarily) be different, too. A true social psychology demands the specification of a more appropriate field of expression. How to do this is the question; one that I shall return to in discussing R. D. Laing's *The Politics of the Family*.

It is possible to characterize Keniston's conceptual model of how alienation occurs as follows: (1) family processes, which lead to (2) individual character traits including that of alienation, all of which is underwritten by (supported by? structured within?—here Keniston is vague) (3) a social structure which is somehow well suited for the existence of both those families and those individuals who are born out of them. Of these three data realms (family, individual, and the larger society) he samples only one intensively (the individual), which obviously weights his whole analysis toward the psychological end. In this light, it is interesting to observe that the data field one would imagine Keniston to be most interested in is that of the family (according to his own analysis, this seems the most important in terms of tracking down the sources of alienation). And yet he does not study the family directly (although, as he makes clear in his references, he is very familiar with the work of his colleagues at

Yale—Theodore Lidz et al.—who have been doing research on the families of schizophrenics for over twenty years).

Keniston's book illustrates a failure of social psychologists in general to develop a coherent conceptual structure for their field which would truly liberate it from psychology and sociology, a conceptual structure which would clearly specify the data realm from which one would want to extract information, which would concretize the nature of the connections between different kinds of facts. The book illustrates a theoretical weakness. Until we have better theory, individual studies will always be inadequate, either through their failure to face real problems or through their inability to illuminate those problems.

EXPERIMENTAL SOCIAL PSYCHOLOGY

We have been looking at an empirical but nonexperimental study which typifies one aspect of the quest by social psychologists for a unifying theoretical scheme which will connect psychology and sociology. Let us turn now to the experimental side of social psychology, to a book which attempts to show us how that experimental social psychology bears on real-world problems. For one of our underlying concerns in this book is analyzing the extent to which social psychology can help formulate a relatively clear view of the complicated issues which lie just beneath the surface of much contemporary discussion and commentary of social problems.

Eliot Aronson's *The Social Animal* is a textbook. Aronson himself is a well-known experimental researcher, and it is his own deep interest in experimental social psychology which informs this text. What is unusual is his capacity to make this difficult often abstruse literature come alive for the beginning student. Aronson connects the different areas of experimental social psychology and makes connections between them and the real world we all live in, the world characterized both by newspaper headlines and common everyday occurrences. He is not simply saying: here is a body of knowledge, take it or leave it; he is saying: here is a fascinating area of research which has important lessons for all of us, for the way we conduct our daily lives, for the way we live.

And yet it is his concern for everyday realities which leads him astray; it leads him away from the strictly experimental vein he had been exploring. His strong fidelity to the realities of everyday life leads him beyond the experimental evidence in a variety of places throughout his book. We shall examine these, for the perplexity of social psychology today is that it has a twofold orientation: toward experimental research carried out according to exacting standards; and also toward the problems of everyday life such as war, riots, poverty, and the complexities of human relations. Yet social psychology lacks that which would enable this connection to be firmly made; only a broad-gauged theory which rises out of or is built on empirical evidence on the one hand, and which yet points to these real-world problems on the other, can make this connection adequately. Meanwhile the experimental evidence that exists—and we are not talking about the other sorts of psychological knowledge, which are considerable—in any field of social psychology, does not bear directly or constantly enough on the problems of our real world such as war and poverty, or personal relations, at least not in a way that anyone can presently perceive. But Aronson tries to connect the experimental evidence to the everyday problems, responding not just out of his divided allegiance (which most social psychologists share) to the experimental on the one hand and the real-world problems on the other, but responding also to the strong current demand for relevance.

Let us take two examples. The first comes from Chapter 7, where Aronson discusses the process of attraction. The way this chapter is constructed is typical of the rest of his chapters. He begins with a thought-provoking discussion of an absorbing topic—why people like each other. Then he reviews various lines of research (and accompanying theories) relevant to this issue; for the most part, this research is experimental. He discusses the reward-cost theory of attraction (one is attracted to someone when the rewards

he gives one outweigh the costs) and makes clear the complexities of the data pertinent to this theory. He reviews
specific lines of research, such as that on physical attractiveness and doing favors as variables which influence
attraction processes. Then, at the end of the chapter, he
again provokes thought by speculation which seems to flow
quite naturally from the experimental evidence. He is talking of authenticity in personal relations, and he speculates
that the more authentic a relationship, the more satisfying
(less boring) it will be. He then talks of what he calls open
and closed relationships, the more open ones being more
authentic, of course, and he links them to a discussion of
plateaus in relationships. His notion is that in a closed
relationship there is less sharing of feelings, and thus a
plateau is reached in the expression of feelings; in an open
relationship more feelings are expressed, both positive and
negative, producing a "zig-zagging of sentiment." He then
says, "In a relationship of this sort, the partners are reasonably close to the gain condition of the gain-loss experiment"
(p. 233). Here he links his speculation about authentic
relations to an earlier experiment he had reviewed, one he
had done to test a gain-loss theory of interpersonal attraction. The point of the experiment and the theory is that
Aronson thinks people will get more pleasure from a given
remark made by another (and have more affection for the
person who makes the remark) if the remark represents an
increase in regard. What matters is not the sheer quantity of
reward provided by the other's nice remarks, but the relationship between his present remarks and his earlier remarks
and attitude. What is interesting is that Aronson goes from
a rather detailed analysis of a single experiment, making
clear its methodological refinements and complexities, implicitly persuading us that a scientist who performs such an
experiment knows what he is doing, to an analysis of a
situation involving authentic relations where there is no
experimental evidence whatsoever. And yet he implicitly
indicates that the earlier experiment on his gain-loss theory
of attraction bears on his later speculation about authentic
relations. In fact, on the face of it, his argument is not

particularly plausible (unless one is determined to believe that authentic relations are better) even within his own theoretical framework.

For a relationship characterized by zigzagging sentiment would produce as much loss as gain presumably; or one might posit a gradually and continually increasing level of reward; the zigzag, that is, would always—over the long run—be moving upward. In order for the overall relationship to be felt as positive, there would have to be some mechanism of a relatively sophisticated sort within us for averaging out these gains and losses in such a way as to make the overall incremental gain seem important. Is this plausible? Who knows? There is certainly no experimental evidence relevant to this issue that I know of.

But more importantly for the present point, Aronson's experimental evidence does not really bear directly on this issue. The issue here is authentic relations: How shall we define them first of all (a conceptual problem)? Second, are they better than nonauthentic relations? And third, why or why not? Aronson implies that his experiment on gains and losses in interpersonal relations bears on this issue, but in fact it does not, at least not in the way he implies; that is, it does not support his argument about the desirability of authentic relations.

CONCEPTUAL ISSUES

This example illustrates the desirability of a more thoroughgoing conceptual analysis (What is authenticity? What do we mean when we talk of authentic relations?) and because it illustrates how the experimental part of social psychology does not lead toward the development of any broad-gauged theory. What might be helpful here is a theory of human relations within which authentic relations would have some kind of place. But what is given instead is a question which appears to have a yes or no answer; that is, are authentic relations better than nonauthentic relations? And the answer here, of course, is yes. What we need to know about authenticity is what it is; and when we have some grasp of that, we can then talk about how it is related to honesty, or self-fulfillment, or the health of the relationship within which authenticity is expressed. And it is these kinds of questions which need to be answered.

Our second example is taken from a chapter on aggression (Chapter 5) where Aronson again goes from general speculation of an interesting nature to a detailed consideration of various lines of experimental research, with the implication that the experimental detail bears directly on the speculation at the beginning. In this chapter he displays not just a general intention to clarify that experimental evidence does bear on important real-life questions, but also a more general bias; in this case, against aggression in its most destructive forms. He clearly wants psychology to have something to tell us all about how to reduce the quantity of harmful human aggression, but the strength of his desire leads him to distort the extent to which the experimental evidence is pertinent to the general problem. In his consideration of aggression, it becomes clearer that the basic problem in social psychology is a conceptual problem, and I want to point out that by and large, Aronson ignores the conceptual dimensions of the problems that social psychology faces.

There are actually two separate but related issues here. The first is the importance of conceptual analysis, of the terms and ideas which are being used. Aronson does not try to examine the idea of authenticity; thus questions arise about whether the definition he presents is the most plausible one, and about how to do a study of authenticity (how one does a study depends in part on how one conceives the initial ideas).

A second issue is a larger one: how ideas are connected into a larger social-psychological theory. Aronson's image of psychology is that of a science with much of importance to say about genuine real-life problems; but until psychology develops a more plausible integrated and articulated conceptual scheme, the research projects that are done will not be related, either to each other or to real-life problems.

Aronson begins this chapter in a sensible fashion, by pointing out examples of aggressive behavior; but then he immediately defines aggression in such a way as to rule out some types of behavior which ordinarily we would call aggression. Thus he goes from examples to a conceptual attempt, but his conceptual attempt does not build on the examples at all; he simply asserts a definition, implying that any definition is suitable so long as we make it clear to one and all. This is conventional procedure in psychology, and has been since the advent of operationalism. The general idea is that terms need clear definitions, and clarity is conceived as what is communicable: if one can repeat another's definition after him to his satisfaction (or if one can use it the way he uses it), then one has a good definition. A good definition is simply one that can be communicated clearly. Needless to say, this procedure slights the whole conceptual end of constructing definitions. It ignores the question whether the definition makes sense, whether it is useful in helping us understand what is being discussed, whether it enables us to make connections with other related phenomena, and so on.

This shying away from serious consideration of conceptual issues is a grave defect in Aronson's text as well as in most of social psychology, and this is a point I shall return to later. However, my interest here is to show that Aronson's definition makes it harder for him to make sense out of real-world phenomena connected with aggression. He defines aggression as "a behavior aimed at causing harm or pain" (p. 143). Of course his definition is selected to make it easier for him to discuss the experimental literature on aggression, but even so, it is not adequate to the data he cites. For example, he talks of an experiment by Michael Kahn (pp. 156-57) in which "a technician taking some physiological measurements from the subjects proceeded to insult and humiliate them." Some subjects were allowed to vent their hostility by expressing it, and "those who were allowed to express the aggression subsequently felt greater dislike and hostility for the technician than did those who were inhibited from expressing the aggression. In other words, expressing aggression did not inhibit the tendency, it tended to increase it." Here Aronson has gone from ex-

pression of aggression (defined as "behavior aimed at causing harm or pain") to *feelings of dislike* for the technician.
Feelings of dislike are then referred to as aggressive tendencies. Aronson has fallen into the everyday habit of referring to feelings of dislike as aggressive, even though in
terms of his definition, dislike cannot be seen as aggressive
(since dislike is not usually intended to cause pain—until
expressed to another, at which point it could be argued that
the intent of the *expression* is to cause pain). This is a small
point, but it makes clear that Aronson's definition does not
illuminate the phenomena of aggression as much as it pre-
tends; what it does is make matters simpler for him, since it
restricts the field of aggression and thus makes it seem more
comprehensible.

Nearly all Aronson's chapters are pervaded by a similar
pattern. He starts with interesting questions; then moves to
experimental evidence (usually not directly pertinent to
answering the interesting questions he begins with); and
then he sometimes ends with interesting speculations,
worded to imply that the preceding experimental evidence
bears on his final speculation. In fact, the evidence does not
in any direct way bear on most of his speculation.

All of this occurs within the context of a general bias
which perhaps many of us share: for peace and harmony and
integration, against war and violence and segregation.
Aronson implies that the experimental evidence (whose
ingenuity and logic he persuades us of while telling us about
it) bears on the larger theoretical questions which of course
interest him and the rest of us social psychologists: What
makes a society cohere? Is war inevitable? Why do men hurt
each other sometimes? And so on. In fact, the experimental
evidence does not do more than faintly illuminate any of
these issues. And this is the dilemma of contemporary social
psychology. We want to be rigorous; we want to be relevant;
but our rigor leads us to do studies which are not, in any
obvious way, germane to the larger social issues of our day.

There are points at which Aronson takes an appropriate
attitude with regard to a difficult question. In talking of
whether or not aggression is instinctive, he points out that

"there is a lack of definite or even clear evidence on the subject of whether or not aggression is instinctive in man" (p. 145). This statement should probably be made about all the difficult problems that Aronson is so interested in. This textbook which introduces the reader to this exciting field, might have performed a greater service if Aronson had been a little more frank about the problems inherent in going from the experimental evidence to the real world. In any science, this is a difficult transition; it is especially difficult in a new one such as social psychology.

BRIEF SUMMARY

In considering these two books in some detail—one a nonexperimental but empirical study by Keniston, and the other a textbook which concentrates on exposition of the experimental portions of social psychology—I have made several points. First, social psychology appears to have no real existence conceptually, although there are certainly people who consider themselves social psychologists, and there are certainly social-psychological studies in abundance. Second, rigorous experimentation in social psychology has not thus far enabled us to construct conceptual schemes which will encompass the rich data provided by the real world around us. Experimentation goes on, but how it is connected within itself and with general theory is by no means clear. Finally, psychologists feel urged to say something relevant about real-world problems, and Aronson's book illustrates one form that urge takes. This eminent experimental social psychologist tries to persuade us that the evidence of experimental research bears quite directly on real-world problems.

To conclude this brief survey of representative aspects of contemporary social psychology, let us turn now to a work by another psychologist who clearly believes that psychology has something important to tell us about real-world problems. Keep in mind that the point of the first chapter is to present a picture of contemporary social psychology: this relatively new science which wants to bridge the gap between psychology and sociology, which wants to attain a certain degree of methodological rigor, and which hopes to contribute to our understanding of contemporary social problems.

SKINNER'S WALDEN TWO

Psychology has become a very popular undergraduate major in liberal arts colleges. The magazine *Psychology Today* has been rather successful lately, and every year best sellers testify to the widespread interest in psychology. Judging from these facts, and from the less explicit but still impressive testimonials rendered by people to someone when they find he is a psychologist (expressions of interest, curiosity, mingled with some trepidation, perhaps), we might guess that people are looking to psychology for some kind of help in understanding themselves and the world they live in.

Psychologists are susceptible to these pleas for help; not just clinical psychologists (whose professional dedication is quite clearly to helping people), but also others. The readiness of psychologists to envision themselves as capable of meeting these expectations is indicated in part by the rapid growth of community psychology in the past decade (a development which extends the therapy model from the treatment of individuals to the treatment of whole communities); it is also indicated by the temptation of psychologists to try to make their work relevant in some striking way. So when B. F. Skinner wrote the novel *Walden Two*, he was to some degree trying, in what has become a rather conventional way, to make his brand of psychological knowledge relevant, to show how his knowledge could be applied to the solving of large social problems. And his novel has been read year after year since he published it in 1948, providing additional evidence about the avidity of Americans for psychological help and knowledge.

But what is curious is that the novel builds so slightly upon the knowledge that Skinner had and has been gathering laboriously in his laboratories in his experiments with—for the most part—pigeons. What we are getting at is not the conventional criticism of Skinner's novel for the lack of relation between research with pigeons and attempts to describe people—a criticism rooted in a belief that pigeons and people are rather different—but another lack of relation: between the novel and Skinner's own scientific principles as elaborated in his more scientific works.

The novel is structured around the visit that Burris, a college professor, makes along with a colleague and four younger people to Walden Two, an experiment in communal living. The visitors are shown around Walden Two by a man named Frazier, and much of the book is taken up with Frazier's attempts to explain what is going on there. The visitors ask questions, and Frazier responds to them with what appear to be Skinner's own ideas about how to set up a more viable social living situation than our own.

BEHAVIORAL ENGINEERING

Frazier's initial point is that Walden Two is based on behavioral engineering. This term is meant to suggest images of laboratory research in which behavior (of animals or people) is controlled by making various kinds of changes in the structure of the stimuli which impinge on the person or animal. Now this is the way Skinner does his experiments with pigeons: the animals are subjected to changing stimuli, and the relationships between these stimuli and the changing behavior are carefully mapped. Skinner quite clearly believes that in principle all of our important behavior can be modified by changing the structure of the external stimuli which impinge on us. However, in his fictitious utopia there is very little evidence of behavioral engineering in this sense, although the term itself is used quite frequently. And the few examples of behavioral engineering which are provided are totally unconnected with Skinner's own behavioristic psychological research; in fact, they seem most similar to the kinds of proposals for changing our daily life which are so numerous in earlier fictional utopias.

There are a number of small engineering details: the

teacups and tea service have been redesigned to make them more practical, but there is nothing to indicate how this change is connected with Skinner's psychology. The teacups seem more connected with conventional American practical know-how and desire to make things more efficient. The tea-service improvement is linked mainly with the tradition of inventions in America; when something does not seem to work very well, we try to invent something better, something more efficient. Similarly, the beds the small children sleep in while very young at Walden Two are an engineering improvement in that they simply seem more practical in the obvious everyday sense of the term. (For some reason, Skinner's promotion of these beds has become a symbol for criticism of his vision, by those who decry the dessication and aridity of the world Skinner wants to impose on the rest of us; the critics see these beds as cutting the child off from the world, even though Skinner makes rather clear in the novel that the beds do not do that at all.) Thus, there are several examples of what we can call plain engineering: not particularly behavioral at all. A good example of this is the work-credit system which he elaborates. This system involves requiring each member of the community to compile a certain number of work credits daily; different kinds of work secure a different number of credits (for each hour worked), depending on how popular and necessary they are. The credits are adjusted every so often, to keep up with changing tastes, in order to make all the necessary work attractive so that people will choose to do even the undesirable work, because so few hours of it have to be done in order to complete the day's work requirements. This system owes nothing in detail to Skinner's own laboratory research, though it does owe a lot to earlier fictional utopias. Characteristically, people who have attempted actually to create communal living arrangements modeled on Skinner's ideas look more to this novel than to his other published scientific research, and use this idea of labor credits, too (such a community in Virginia, called Twin Oaks, is described in Kathleen Kinkade's *A Walden Two Experiment*).

There is, however, one real example of behavioral engineering that clearly derives from Skinner's kind of behavioristic psychology: the teaching of frustration tolerance to the children. Here psychology comes explicitly into play. The child is given small tasks at first, then gradually larger ones, all of them involving some degree of frustration. The objective is to teach the child to tolerate frustration. Skinner may think that frustration is an inevitable part of life and that much contemporary malaise derives from people who cannot tolerate frustration. But no matter what the underlying ideology (and Skinner leaves it vague), the method of teaching frustration tolerance is clearly behavioristic in Skinner's sense; and the idea that frustration tolerance is important is a generally psychological idea (not specifically behavioristic, of course). Skinner evades the question of what happens when people—because of the success of their education in frustration tolerance—lose their ability to recognize frustrations which should not be tolerated, which is very strange, since the whole motivation for writing his novel is his own perception that contemporary life is more frustrating than is necessary.

We said that the novel is built only slightly on the findings of behavioristic psychology; even when Skinner does give an example of using behavioristic psychology (as he does in this teaching of frustration tolerance) he fails to connect this specifically behavioral molding with the rest of his communal arrangements. In Chapter 14 of his novel we see how the child is taught frustration tolerance; then we move on to another topic, and the example of frustration tolerance is left behind.

EXPERIMENTATION

Frazier refers to Walden Two as an experiment, and one of the ways in which the author tries to convince us that this community is indeed founded on scientific principles is the frequent repetition of the experiment motif. Frazier says that often experiments are done to find out what works best: for example, to find out whether married couples should live together or not, some newly married couples were randomly selected (at the beginning of Walden Two's existence) and divided into two groups. In one group, husbands and wives had separate rooms, and in the other group they did not; after eight years of this, tests were done to assess the happiness, compatibility, and mutual satisfaction of the various husbands and wives. The couples who had separate rooms scored much higher than the others on the various tests, Frazier says, and so now all couples are provided with separate rooms to use if they like.

In this experiment several points are important. First, it owes nothing specifically to behavioristic psychology; it is simply modeled on the general scientific principle of gathering facts in order to answer questions. Second, it is not an experiment in the rigorous sense, since too many variables are left uncontrolled. Finally, the experiment is very vague on the crucial facts: What were the tests? The underlying assumption (which perhaps most people share) is that when psychologists want to find out whether someone is happy, they can give a test, and then they know. This assumption is somewhat misleading, to say the least, although one cannot be certain to what extent Skinner appreciates this, since his own research (needless to say) does not indulge in tests of happiness. This is not the only place in his novel where Skinner paints a picture of a psychologist who is able to tell what is best for people by talking with them or by doing routine clinical assessment. For example, in Chapter 16, where he is discussing marriage and childbearing, he makes clear that "When a young couple become engaged, they go to our Manager of Marriages. Their interests, school records, and health are examined. If there's any great discrepancy in intellectual ability or temperament they are advised against marrying" (p. 135). This is either an expression of ignorance on Skinner's part (of the complexity of the assessment of future compatibility in a young couple), or it is an attempt on his part to contribute to the popular mythology which sees the psychologist as possessed of extraordinary powers of divination. Either way, the invocation of the psychologist's powers here has nothing to do with Skinner's brand of behavioral psychology; thus, even in places where Skinner explicitly refers to psychological knowledge, it is not at all clear that he is referring to the sort of knowledge he himself has been most effective in gathering.

Some of his remarks about the family and the role of women are interesting in the light of contemporary concern for sexual equality. Skinner here (and elsewhere in the book) makes many sound comments on deficiencies in our present society, as when he points out that the marriage system trades on feelings of insecurity in women; and further, that of course women are the hardest to convince of the virtues of the new communal child-rearing ethic at Walden Two, because women—like exploited workers—are kept in their place "not by external force, but much more subtly by a system of beliefs implanted within their skins" (p. 148).

But however pleasing this statement may sound to some contemporary ears, it is jarring in the context of the book. Why? Because the lack of connection between this particular ideology (in favor of sexual equality) and the psychological methods employed in Walden Two raises the possibility that the psychological methods proposed in the novel could be used in the service of any ideology. (This, of course, is one reason this novel has disturbed so many people so much.) Skinner defeats his own purpose by failing to connect the ideology (of equality, etc.) in the novel with the psychology. He tries to imply that the ideology is the psychology, but obviously that is not the case.

This statement is interesting for a further reason. Skinner refers to a system of beliefs implanted within a person. But how would this come about? Skinner provides no original analysis of this question. He conjures up visions of brainwashing similar to those evoked by Hunter in his sensational book on that topic twenty years ago.[4] But any psychologist who has read the more careful studies of coercive persuasion (as Schein calls it) knows that there is nothing easy about consciously and conscientiously implanting a

4. Edward Hunter, *Brainwashing in Red China* (New York: Vanguard Press, 1951).

system of beliefs in the head of someone else. Of course psychologists take for granted that each culture has ways of leading people to think certain things; but every culture has iconoclasts; and the mystery of course is how exactly each of us acquires the set of beliefs we happen to have by the time we are twenty or twenty-five years old. Psychologists have general answers to these questions; but the behavioral psychologists have made no concrete contributions to this area of research other than to make widespread the use of the word *conditioning*, which most people seem to take to mean that psychologists know how to implant ideas in peoples' minds. But this is far from the truth.

THE USE OF HISTORY

One of the curious contradictions of *Walden Two* is the way in which Frazier repeats that history teaches us nothing, that only experimentation gives us reliable knowledge; historical events do not constitute experiments, and so give us no sure knowledge about what happened—its inevitability, and the like. He argues further that what passes for historical fact is actually historical interpretation. This is not so startling a position for an experimental scientist to take. But then Frazier turns around and argues that one of the principal reasons to think that an experiment like Walden Two, with many unusual living arrangements, is worth trying, is that past experience indicates that our present ways of doing things are not working and are therefore not workable. Of course, this is an appeal to history; he is saying that history shows that certain arrangements do not work (the usual family arrangements for raising children, for example), and therefore we should try something new. If you really cannot trust history, then as a psychologist you can trust only experimental evidence. And yet there is no experimental evidence which bears directly on the issue he is discussing (how to raise children: in communal nurseries, in the family, etc.).

This contradiction gets at one part of the central problem of *Walden Two:* Skinner attempts to persuade us that psychological research has important knowledge for us all about how to live, but in fact the novel does not persuade us of that at all. The novel is predicated on an exaggerated estimation of the relevance of experimental psychology for the conduct of everyday life, and the vagueness of the references to psychological research betrays this. This should be no surprise, for it is indeed difficult to go from isolated pigeons in a box to a society of people, and Skinner has as hard a time making that transition as any of us would.

BRIEF REVIEW

In this first chapter, I have examined certain key features of contemporary social psychology. Certain key texts have served as reference points for discussion, but the intention has been to focus the reader's attention not on these texts themselves, but on the ideas which animate them, and on the picture of social psychology which they imply. The general theme is that social psychologists have large ambitions, unfulfilled for lack of a conceptual framework within which empirical research might fit, and with the aid of which one might comprehend at least something of the dynamics and structure of the relationships between an individual and society.

Social psychology tries to integrate sociology and psychology; some of the difficulties of this attempt are seen in Keniston's *The Uncommitted*. Although it tries to combine sociological and psychological approaches, it has the conceptual weaknesses which are endemic to social psychology. And this is the important point: social psychology cannot come into existence on its own until it attains a conceptual basis. Much of the rest of this book is devoted to trying to articulate what that conceptual basis might be. Have the high hopes of social psychology for a combination of methodological rigor and social relevance been fulfilled? Although there are many carefully-worked-out experimental approaches to social psychological issues, these approaches do not necessarily and inevitably, taken by themselves, accumulate so as to illuminate general social problems. What is necessary, if this kind of accumulation is to be illuminating, is that these experiments fit together in some kind of more general theoretical framework. But thus far, most experimental approaches in social psychology arise piecemeal, out of some combination of a researcher's interests and the state of previous experimentation on a given topic. Occasionally there are research programs where many experiments are done within the context of a general concern (such as the Yale attitude-change studies of Hovland et al.); but even here, the inability to place the results of these experiments within a general theory of human nature and sociality suggests that their implications for our general understanding of man in society cannot be confidently shown.

Finally, I have considered the general appeal which psychology has today, the way in which people look to psychologists for answers to their pressing problems, and the ways in which psychologists try to respond to these pressures. Specifically, Skinner's *Walden Two* illustrates the difficulty in going from one body of psychological knowledge to a general picture of man's relation to society. The principal difficulty is a dearth of general ideas of persuasive integrative power. Specific experiments do not provide such ideas; the ideas must come from elsewhere, of course, and experiments are designed usually to try to eliminate the misleading aspects of our conceptions about how people work. The experimental approach is necessary, beyond any doubt; but it will not by itself lead to the kind of general picture we need if we are to satisfactorily confront the general problems which beset us when we try to understand general social events.

How are we to obtain the kind of general theoretical scheme which will enable us to make social psychology a true science in its own right, to comprehend the various experimental and other empirical studies which have been done, and to cast light on general social problems? There is no easy answer (if there were, this book would not be necessary).

By examining the work of several important writers, and

looking for connections, we can find at least the rudiments of an admittedly tentative and fragmentary but nonetheless helpful picture of how man can be conceived as fitting into society. A consideration now of one example of a critical analysis of our society—of our high schools—will spell out the crucial elements in one kind of critical stance vis-à-vis our society. Once we have this critical position in view because it is influential and important, we shall see how social psychology can be construed as helping us evaluate it. For one aim of this book is to show how social psychology can contribute something important to public debate about general social issues.

CHAPTER 2

Social Criticism:
A Critical Analysis of a Social
Institution

What social psychological ideas are available to help us understand some of the perplexities of contemporary discussion of social problems? Even though the experimental end of psychology is difficult to apply directly to such an understanding, at least at the present time, there are a number of ideas in social psychology which can help us place some social problems within a context, and to see through and around some of the contemporary popular analysis of these social problems. One such social problem is the dissatisfaction with educational institutions in America, on the part of both students and others who feel that the educational system does not fulfill its high ideals, or perhaps fulfills some rather low ideals all too well.

Respectable radical criticism (as I shall refer to it here) provides the backbone of many of the critical analyses of our contemporary social institutions. The educational system in America comes in for rather sharp criticism, some of which is both radical and respectable at the same time. It is radical in that it is sweeping and sharp; wholesale indictments are often the order of the day. And it is respectable in that many people who appear to be living in the midst of the system rather comfortably seem able to assume the critical stance provided in these analyses without any great appearance of discomfort.

A critical analysis of a social institution such as the educational system is only possible if one has at least some social-psychological notions, however fragmentary and tenuous. One must have some concepts which describe the structure of the institution, and some which refer to the effects of that structure on human beings. Most critical analyses of our educational structure which are radical—in that they offer sweeping indictments—are not very specific with regard to their fundamental assumptions, with regard to their conceptual structure. However, if one dissects them, he can find some of that fundamental underlying conceptual structure. Since the point of this book is not to dismantle certain radical criticisms of our social institutions, but rather to construct the basis for a truly social-psychological critical evaluation and understanding of our society, there will be no prolonged attempt to survey all the criticisms of our educational system. One fairly typical critical analysis will be taken for illustration. No evidence can be offered here as to how "typical" this particular critical analysis is; but the shape of the argument does not hinge on this, for the point is simply to show how one appraisal of one of our social institutions falls short of its goal of providing a clear understanding of that institution.

The article by Paul Lauter and Florence Howe, "How the School System Is Rigged for Failure," [1] will be a reference point. It contains respectable radical analysis of the sort which has become so popular in the past decade or so. The ultimate aim is to compare the thinking contained in this article with the kind of grasp of social-psychological problems we can construct from the thought of various social theorists yet to be considered.

1. In the *New York Review of Books*, June 18, 1970, pp. 14-21.

THE CRITICAL POINT OF VIEW

Although in their article, various arguments are woven together, there are three main themes. After discussing each in turn, I shall consider the coherence and power of the whole analysis, although inevitably some evaluation of the separate arguments will be made earlier.

(1) The schools do not eliminate poverty, nor promote mobility, but rather maintain the unhappy status quo. This is Lauter and Howe's first point. They begin by pointing out that Americans have traditionally had high hopes for their schools. One of these high hopes has been that schools will help to eliminate poverty and will teach certain basic skills, such as reading, writing, and arithmetic. They then show that the schools do not succeed in these aims; and finally—this is the critical part—conclude that the schools have never really intended to succeed, the schools maintain the status quo. The schools intend to fail, and do fail quite successfully (fail to impart much knowledge in some cases; fail to eliminate poverty, and so on).

Reduced to its simplest form, the authors' argument goes from (a) the fact that schools were established, as part of our national public policy, by people who said that the intention of the schools is to eliminate poverty and teach basic skills and thus increase social mobility; to (b) the fact that poverty still exists in America today, and social mobility seems either nonexistent or rather minimal; and conclude (c) that the schools must not really be run to eliminate poverty or to teach basic skills. This critical train of thought has several underlying assumptions. One is that any social institution—such as the educational system—serves a function. Another is that the function can be identified with what appears to be the result of the system. If the schools do not eliminate poverty, if they do not impart much wisdom, that must be because it is their function *not* to do so. This form of argument takes anything that looks like malfunctioning on the surface, and states that actually, when the surface is probed and what is underneath is laid bare, one will see that the apparent malfunctioning is only apparent; in reality, the social system is healthy and functioning very well indeed.

The logic in this kind of argument is clear; pushed to an extreme, of course, the logic collapses insofar as it refuses to consider malfunctioning as a real possibility so far as societal institutions are concerned, because this logic puts examples of apparent malfunctioning into the category of covert functioning, which becomes difficult to defend. At the extreme, this argument refuses to recognize the possibility of malfunctioning in a social system.

This kind of argument is quite respectable and has been made over and over again; in a sense, Marx and Freud have given the major modern impetus to this form of argument. Thus, in many fields, we have all encountered the argument that things are not what they seem, that they are actually the opposite of what they seem. The great problem with regard to this argument lies in its versatility. It can be used too widely; it can seem to pertain to everything. Insofar as its scope is limitless, insofar as the kinds of evidence necessary to support it are never specified, it loses its value. Thomas Szasz has gone to a lot of trouble to point out, in great detail, the difficulties which Freudian theory encounters in making this kind of argument about individual human malfunctioning. His argument (briefly, and only in part) is that Freud erred in collapsing the perfectly useful category of malfunctioning on the individual human level, into the category of illness (see *The Myth of Mental Illness*).

This analysis of our schools says that they are failing to end poverty, that this represents a success (they are trying not to end it), and that this is bad. The last conclusion—that this state of affairs is bad—owes its energy to the assumption that schools could indeed end poverty if the people who run the schools wanted them to do so.

This assumption seems questionable. Lauter and Howe are doubtless right that Americans have always had high hopes for their schools, but we can question whether these hopes have ever been realistic. One of the bewildering characteristics of much contemporary radical criticism of America is that it seems to partake as much as does ordinary nonradical thinking of typical American attitudes, principal among which is a kind of overwhelming optimism. This is bewildering partly perhaps because one expects to find radical thinking different from other more conventional kinds of thinking; but, in fact, much radical thought in America partakes of the deeply conventional American belief in perfectibility, fundamentally a form of chronic optimism. The Lauter and Howe attack on our schools for not eliminating poverty is neither more nor less bizarre than that aspect of American ideology which holds that schools could and should eliminate poverty.

The high school is portrayed as very good at maintaining the status quo. The impression conveyed is that it never fails at this; it is inevitably successful. The underlying fantasy (for so it seems) is that the educational system is supercompetent, doing relentlessly what it is designed (covertly, but intentionally) to do. This is a hard argument to maintain, since so far no social system has been that competent.

No social subsystem—whether an educational system, a political system, or whatever—does perfectly what it is designed to do. There are always gaps between the goals and the attainments. The image of any social system as supercompetent may be based in part on being or feeling outside the system. Working inside any social system is one fairly sure way to acquire information and understanding which make clear that the system does not work very well some of the time. Further, no social system is homogeneous. Social systems have competing forces within them (although appreciating that from a position outside the system is difficult).

Or it may be that seeing social systems as homogeneous and supercompetent is fueled by the wish to have perfect (serene and unconflicted and competent) social institutions. One problem with the idea of a perfect social institution is that it does not leave room for change. Change arises in part out of a situation where there are conflicting forces. If there are no conflicting forces, there is no possibility of the germs of change taking root and growing.

At this point, we must concede the theoretical possibility that a subsystem of a given society might be homogeneous, even though the total society cannot be. Thus, Lauter and Howe might argue that the educational social structure is homogeneous: no change can arise from it, and any change which is going to occur will have to be imposed from outside. On a theoretical level, this seems a tenable argument.

(2) Some people in the schools have more power than others. This is bad, for they use it to keep other people down. Lauter and Howe see certain unhealthy aspects of our present social reality (poverty, ignorance, etc.) as deriving from or as part of the school system. But furthermore, they attribute this to malevolent intentions on the part of those who run the schools. Thus, much of their argument consists in trying to show how what the school does is actually designed by a particular group of people to keep other people down. For example, Lauter and Howe see the providing of vocational training as shunting lower-class children away from the middle-class way of life. They imply that having the opportunity to attain a middle-class way of life would be a good thing for lower-class children, although there are many other points in their article where they state their contempt for (or reservations about) the middle-class way of life. Similarly, they see any insistence on order and discipline in the schools as a way of (a) providing business with well-trained recruits after school is finished; and (b) keeping lower-class children from getting into business and other middle-class pursuits, because they will not be able to tolerate the imposition of discipline and the rules of order so well as the middle-class children.

These arguments see malevolent intentions as underlying the way the school operates. What the school actually does (provide vocational training, or insist that children come to school on time) is interpreted as reflecting the intentions of someone (so far unspecified) to do others harm. The students who get the vocational training are by and large the lower-class students; thus these students are *not* being offered a good opportunity to climb out of the lower class by learning the skills necessary to go on to college and a (presumably) middle-class career. The diagnosis of malevolence rides on the shared assumption that, in the cases just mentioned, staying lower-class is bad, or that doing well in business (by being punctual) is bad. A further assumption is that lower-class means poor, although this is a tangled issue, for some vocational training, although leading to a kind of career referred to as lower-class does not necessarily lead to poverty; and as C. Wright Mills among others has made clear (in his *White Collar*), becoming what sociologists would call middle-class is not necessarily preferable to being what sociologists would call lower-class.

There is no clear-cut way to prove the authors' argument wrong; but at the same time, there is no clear-cut way to figure out how to gather evidence and evaluate its accuracy. One wonders whether evidence for their view is more persuasive than that for various alternative views. Staying within the functionalist framework, for example, we might argue that a given practice (insisting on a certain amount of order or discipline in a school, or trying to set up a vocational training program) has multiple functions. How should one gather evidence about which one or many functions a given custom or practice serves?

There are two issues here, both of them fundamental to contemporary social psychology. First, one must show how evidence can be derived which bears on one's views. Ideally, of course, one will gather that evidence, but if that is difficult, at least pointing out where and how the evidence can be accumulated is important. Second, one must formulate alternative explanations and weigh them against the favored explanation. One of the aims of research and theory in social psychology is excluding alternative explanations of whatever phenomenon one is studying.

So far as the issue of evidence goes, Lauter and Howe do attempt to provide some evidence for their specific points; for example, with regard to the argument that the schools exist to provide discipline and order to produce well-trained recruits for business, they adduce the fact that a Harris poll reveals that 62 percent of parents questioned think that in school maintaining discipline is more important than student self-inquiry.

But this raises more problems than it settles. First, such specific evidence is by no means relevant to their general assumption, that school practices serve functions which involve maintaining the status quo (to attempt to formulate what seems to be their most general assumption). Second, the fact is not really relevant to their specific point. They want to argue, it seems, not that discipline is important in school, but rather that they know *why* discipline is important in schools. They want to convince us that discipline is important in schools not because teachers feel that students should be able to hear themselves think, or not because parents feel guilty about not being able to be firm at home themselves and are therefore sticking the school with the burdens of instilling a sense of discipline into their children. They want to argue instead that the function of discipline in the schools is to provide recruits for business who will be able to show up on time for work, who will be able to follow orders. The fact they cite—from the Harris poll—is not relevant to this issue at all, and its inclusion serves only to confuse the issue. That is, the fact they adduce does not help them prove that their explanation of the phenomenon of discipline in school is correct.

Further, some confusion derives from their hidden assumption that imposing discipline as a major task of the school system is the work of a small elite group which benefits from this imposition. If it in fact turns out that more than half the parents are in favor of this kind of discipline in the schools, it implies either that the elite groups insisting that the schools impose discipline is not so small after all, or it implies that the small elite group has not only taken over the schools, but taken over the minds of people in general. This latter of course is a very popular idea, made most persuasive by Marcuse perhaps (in his *One-Dimensional Man*), and quite possibly Lauter and Howe subscribe to this idea. I shall consider Marcuse's argument in some detail later.

Lauter and Howe's use of the term *national interest* is interesting insofar as it appears to be derogatory: they seem to see it covering a situation where a rich powerful few benefit. For example, " ... tracking is to schools what channeling is in the draft. The function is identical, namely, the control of manpower 'in the National Interest.' " They put the phrase "in the National Interest" in quotes perhaps to indicate that what some people—government planners, for example—call the national interest is in fact the interest of a very few rich powerful people, an elite. The implication here, and also in the repeated use of the term *educational system*, is that there is an elite which benefits from the way society runs, and a large group of oppressed people who do not benefit, who in fact lose. Sometimes it seems that their elite is the white middle class—in which case it is not a small elite, of course, but rather large. This is a critical point: are they implying that there is a small elite (say 20 percent of the members of a society) keeping everyone else (the other 80 percent) down? Most of the language and conceptual theory which support a view of society made of warring classes derives from a situation where there was a relatively small elite and a relatively large oppressed majority. To take this way of thinking and apply it to a situation where there may be a large group (the entire middle class of America) keeping a smaller group (the poor) down, is not so simple.

This point is interesting since the underlying objection to the predominance of the middle class in our high schools seems to be the moral indignation experienced by some at the fact that some people do things for their own benefit. The respectable radical criticism seems to hold up, as a goal, an implicit image of a society where people will not do things for their own benefit. By criticizing a situation where they say some people (the middle class) are arranging things so that they will benefit more than others, they imply that in a better society, either (a) no one will be in control, or (b) the people in control will not systematically do things for their own benefit.

Both these ideas are problematic. The latter implies a new kind of man who places the interests of others on an even level with his own interests. This has been an ideal in our civilization for centuries; it is one aspect of the Judeo-Christian ideology, and as such is deeply planted. The Lauter and Howe argument however does not discuss the issues of whether the creation of a new kind of person is possible or necessary for a new society. Instead, they confine themselves to objecting to the present system; by so confining themselves, they imply that if only we could change the people in charge (get the middle classes out of control), society would change in important ways. This is not, on the face of it, a tenable assumption, although it may be tenable if the proper arguments can be mustered.

One part of the authors' indictment of society is that they view opportunities as limited. This indictment presupposes the possibility that a society might exist where opportunities are not limited. This presumption is as much a part of American mythology as the one they ridicule (the simplistic belief that opportunities are unlimited in our present society). Their form of this belief seems to involve asserting that opportunities are limited in our society now only because of an evil group—identified loosely by Lauter and Howe as the white middle class. The implication is that once this group is gotten out of the way (or out of control), then opportunities will be unlimited. This might well be a delusion. Opportunities might, in fact, be limited in any society for each member of that society, depending on place of birth, parents, the immediate social group, the economic conditions at the time of birth, and the like. It may be that we are all limited by our environments (as well as we are given unique opportunities by our environments). This is difficult for us to believe, and the radical ideologues are as American as those they despise in their assumption that unlimited opportunity is a real possibility for every member of a society.

Another pervasive assumption in this kind of thinking is that people should be equal—not just in the eyes of the law, but in abilities and motivations. Thus, any indication that people are not equal in our present society is taken as evidence of malign social forces rather than of the possibility that the people are not equal for some other reason (by virtue of the operation of social forces which are neither malign or benign but simply there; or because people are somewhat different at birth' and go through different life experiences, interacting with different people, this latter interactional process possibly being too complicated to be accounted for by any simple theory of inequality or individual differences deriving from an image of bad people pushing others around).

The kind of argument Lauter and Howe make is simple: one identifies two different-seeming social groups (men and women, or blacks and whites), and then examines whether these two groups are differentially present in some situation (an occupational category such as that of nuclear physicist, where there are mostly men and very few women; or a situational category like that of The Bronx High School of Science, where there are mostly whites and very few non-whites). When one finds that the two groups are differentially represented in the situation or occupation, one then concludes that this situation arises because of some powerful group which uses its power to keep some people down and out. However, the possibility is never considered that there may be societal forces independent of those arising out of bad powerful elite groups of individuals which operate so as to produce the given result. Society may be more complicated than a simple picture of class warfare indicates, especially the grossly oversimplified picture of class warfare where one class is identified as good and the other as bad, where one is the oppressor and the other the oppressed. In some societal situations, the oppressor-oppressed dichotomy makes some sense and leads to some kind of understanding of the situation. This is especially true in societies where there is a relatively small group of powerful people which is relatively homogeneous and relatively cohesive, unburdened by any responsibility for their actions. There is evidence that in certain sectors of our society such groups exist, but the evidence is far from being clear-cut; and it is not obvious at all how this evidence is linked to the Lauter and Howe analysis of the high schools. The work of Thomas

Schelling is relevant here, and in Chapter 7 I shall consider it in some detail.

Some of Freud's thinking is pertinent as well. One of Freud's contributions is to clarify the impact we older human beings have on other younger human beings (here is what appears to be an unavoidable inequality, at the root of human life as it were). A newborn baby is relatively helpless; that is a fairly clear fact. Freud has helped us see the ways in which, through doing the necessary helping that infants require to live, we adults influence them. The influence is very subtle, and in some ways perhaps inevitably unfortunate. However, escaping the influence seems—given our current knowledge of biology and psychology—impossible. At present, newborn babies need help to survive; and the help they get is always contaminated by various kinds of structured communications and pressures, all of which lead the child in some directions rather than others. Freud makes fairly clear that by the time the baby is old enough to know he is being led in one direction rather than another, he is already hooked; try as he may, he will never entirely escape those earlier influences. The work of Laing constitutes an examination of this issue, as we shall see later.

Doubtless, there are ways to reduce the malign influences which the adults effect. But there seem no easy ways. The structure of the situation is not that easily changed; one cannot simply decry the social reality and say "let us make it different," in order for it to become different. Something more is required. In part, what we need is a more adequate theory than we now possess of the relationship between society and the individual. This is the issue which will occupy us in much of the remainder of this book.

3. People are hurt by the system. An important thread of Lauter and Howe's entire argument is that people in general are hurt by the present system, not just in the sense that out-groups are victimized by an in-group, but in the sense that there is something destructive about the system which affects everyone involved in it. Here the authors seem to make two related points: (a) that the social system pushes people around and, by implication, that this is avoidable;

and (b) that people's own needs are not fulfilled in society at present, for society forces people to fulfill its ends instead. Underlying both these ideas is a simple dichotomization of society separate from the individual. Only if the individual is seen separate from the society can he be seen as being pushed around by it and frustrated because of it.

In their unhappiness with channeling and streaming devices (in the high schools and in society at large), the authors seem to assume that any situation in which societal structures and forces push individual people in one direction rather than another is undesirable. They fail to recognize at least the possibility that any social structure is going to push people one way rather than another. Insofar as a society has structure, it is going to make doing some things easier than others. The idea that any individual in a society larger than one will have total freedom—to do what he wants, and not to do what he does not want to do—is very possibly a delusion. The real question seems to be not whether a particular individual is being led, subtly or very forcibly, to do something which he might not want to do with his whole spontaneous heart, but rather the relationship between the things he wants to do and the things he is led or forced to do; and further, the relationship between the society's goals and the way in which it achieves them.

The underlying feeling is one of outrage that society should have mechanisms which enable it to go on existing, mechanisms which inevitably restrict the movements of individuals within it. This outrage seems to derive from a truly radical belief in the sacredness of the individual, a belief which is of course typically American. Given this assumption, any kind of societal planning seems evil because it restricts the individual's freedom in one way or another. This is an important theme of radical thought—both right and left—in America. Relevant here are interesting studies of American literature which show, as central themes running throughout American literature of the past two hundred years, the attempt to escape the social world surrounding all of us, or the attempt to create a self which, by expansion, will become imperial and will exercise dominion over all the world (see, for example, Richard Poirier's *A World Elsewhere,* or Quentin Anderson's *The Imperial Self*).

An example of the moral piety, separated from critical consciousness (or whatever a more analytical attitude should be called) which is so common, is the last sentence of the Lauter and Howe article, which implies that the authors prefer a school system which instead of perpetuating privilege "would permit children to develop according to their own needs and abilities" (p. 21). This is moral piety: it appeals to our moral sensibilities in a way that prevents us from disagreeing. All of us, reading this, would say amen. *But*—this is the problem of course—how does one set up a situation so that children can develop according to their own needs, given (a) that older people have more psychological and social power than younger ones (especially more than children who are between 2 and 12 or so); and (b) that ascertaining true needs as opposed to false ones is a very complicated task? One's needs are inordinately complicated; figuring out which ones to develop may not be easy.

Let us try to understand this. When we say that adults have more power than children, we simply are drawing attention to that feature of any society where adults impose themselves and their visions of reality on younger people. How it can be otherwise is the question. How do you raise a child without to some extent affecting him and making him different from what he was to begin with; and how do you ever ascertain with any degree of certainty that you are helping the child through this process to follow his own bent? This question leads directly into the second point just made: how does one know a true bent or need or aptitude or whatever from a false one in oneself or in another?

Adult people in different societies have different needs, and that these needs are not haphazardly related to the society is obvious. Even the so-called deviant needs in any given society are not haphazard with respect to the society in which they flower. Given this fact, and given the obvious paucity of evidence about the true needs of infants, how can one argue that it is possible with any degree of confidence to set up a system to ensure that children will follow their own needs? What is an *own need?* How does one know what one needs? And even if there is a way to answer this question for oneself, how does one answer it for others, especially such an other as an infant human being?

Ordinarily, when we reflect on the ways in which society prevents each of us from fulfilling our own needs, we are making a very simpleminded distinction between what we think, at a given moment, we really want (to read a book, play golf, listen to music, bake a pie, or whatever) and what we have to do because of our job or whatever (go to work, take care of a baby, etc.). Obviously, each of us can at a given moment discern multiple needs: to retain the respect and income that come from the job, to avoid the guilt which might come from not going to work, to gain the pleasure that comes from listening to music, to avoid the boredom that comes from not having anything to do which interests us. But does this elementary fact about human psychology—which observes the presence of multiple and contradictory needs in each of us—necessarily prove that some of these needs are real and genuine and natural, and others are false and unreal and nongenuine? Not necessarily. It is relatively easy to argue persuasively that all the needs of any adult have a social (artificial, taught, not innate) character. And even in young children, many of the needs manifested have a social component.

In addition to the conceptual problem—trying to resolve how one is going to differentiate false from true needs on a conceptual level—there is a psychological problem; each of us has great difficulty trying to ascertain our true needs. For example, when I want to go to a movie and read a book and talk with a friend, which of these is really my true need at the moment? This is a psychological problem: no matter how many theoretical distinctions we draw between true and false needs, I will still be faced with the concrete phenomenological task (or whatever it should be called) of figuring out, when I am aware of a number of needs, which represents my true need. It is distinctly possible that there is, in such a situation, no one true need. Perhaps there are instead a *number* of needs, all equally true (or false); then one must *decide* which to indulge or follow or live, and this decision may not in any given case do more to fulfill one's true needs than any other decision. One need not be an existentialist philosopher or psychiatrist to find this an interesting problem (although they discuss it more than other writers do); however, Lauter and Howe and other radical ideologues ignore this question. Marcuse makes more clear than anyone else the problems one gets into in trying to differentiate false from true needs, and although he seems relatively thoughtful in examining this issue, many radical ideologues have taken his (and Marx's, etc.) distinction between false and true needs and simply accepted it uncritically. Of course, adding Freud's distinctions between conscious and unconscious needs only makes the problems here vastly more complicated.

THE COHERENCE AND POWER OF THE LAUTER AND HOWE ANALYSIS

We have been reviewing various themes which run through one critical analysis of the contemporary social institutions of education. We have attempted to concentrate mainly on exposition of the themes of the argument, although inevitably we have also begun the task which will preoccupy us in this book: to construct some kind of more adequate social-psychological theory than that which informs this kind of critical analysis. So when the critical analysis decries a situation in which people suffer, we ask whether their concept of suffering (in this case, that people's own needs are not being gratified) is adequate. And we have begun searching for a more adequate conceptual structure which will help us to see the relation of individual and society. Before continuing with that project, let us evaluate the scope and power of the conceptual structure we have been examining.

(1) The authors' analysis of conformity and alternative analyses. The authors argue that the schools teach only

conformity. (They would probably argue that all of our social institutions teach conformity.) In order seriously to maintain this line of argument, one must explain away all the nonconformists of the world who went to school. Lauter and Howe themselves for example, presumably see themselves as nonconformists—at least verbally, as in this article—and they presumably went to school. They can retort that they are accidents; that all the nonconformists who emerge from the schools emerge in spite of the schools. But this is exactly the form of argument that they try to demolish; earlier they were arguing that *what is* (whether it is poverty or illiteracy or whatever social evil we care to name) exists not as an accidental by-product but because it is produced by or sustained by the system. Similarly, ought they not argue that nonconformity exists because it is produced by the system? That seems to be a reasonable enough argument, although hard to prove.

Lauter and Howe could try another line of argument, claiming that what looks like nonconformity (that which leads us to say look, there are many nonconformists in the world) is not really nonconformity. That gets them deeper into their "all that is, is evil" argument, and it makes their own position in this society (writing such an article as this, publishing it, presumably hoping that people will read it and agree with them) somewhat tenuous. If we are all conformists, why bother with this article?

With regard to the issue of where conformity comes from, and how the schools are connected with it, the interpretation which arises from the thought of some of the social psychological thinkers we shall be examining later is that any society is concerned with conformity. Any situation in which people are living together at relatively close quarters is going to generate forces toward conformity. But so long as people are different, so long as teachers with divergent viewpoints are hired, so long as there is no way of making sure that everyone does exactly the same thing, inevitably there are going to be forces which generate nonconformity in terms of the system, however the system is defined. The problem is to identify the forces which tend to produce conformity and the opposing forces which produce nonconformity, and then to identify the social structures which generate each type of force.

On the face of it, arguing that nonconformity is generated by the system is as tenable as arguing that conformity is generated by the system. Goffman makes this argument, and although we shall consider his work in some detail later, it is worth raising this point here. He argues in *Asylums* that:

> The practice of reserving something of oneself from the clutch of an institution is very visible in mental hospitals and prisons but can be found in more benign and less totalistic institutions, too. I want to argue that this recalcitrance is not an incidental mechanism of defense but rather an essential constituent of the self.
>
> Sociologists have always had a vested interest in pointing to the ways in which the individual is formed by groups, identifies with groups, and wilts away unless he obtains emotional support from groups. But when we closely observe what goes on in a social role, a spate of sociable interaction, a social establishment—or in any other unit of social organization—embracement of the unit is not all that we see. We always find the individual employing methods to keep some distance, some elbow room, between himself and that with which others assume he should be identified . . . perhaps we should . . . initially define the individual, for sociological purposes, as a stance-taking entity, as something that takes up a position somewhere between identification with an organization and opposition to it . . . it is thus *against something* that the self can emerge (pp. 319-20, author's italics).

Goffman's argument is not persuasive without more detail which will be supplied later, but it illustrates that one can argue plausibly that nonconformity is generated by a social system.

Another form of argument makes its analysis not at the level of individual behavior—does he conform to the system or not—but at the level of structural analysis of an entire social system. Marx provided a conceptual analysis of social structure which posited class conflict as a basic element of social organization. Thus, Ralf Dahrendorf's interesting discussion of class conflict (in his book *Class and Class Conflict in Industrial Society*) contains the following:

> For Marx, society is not primarily a smoothly functioning order of the form of a social organism, a social system, or a static social fabric. Its dominant characteristic is, rather, the continuous change of not only its elements, but its very structural form. This change in turn bears witness to the presence of conflicts as an essential feature of every society. Conflicts are not random; they are a systematic product of the structure of society itself (p. 27).

Dahrendorf's basic topic is exactly the fact that conflict is produced within and by any society:

> I am concerned with a problem, namely, with the puzzling fact that social structures as distinct from most other structures are capable of producing within themselves the elements of their supersession and change. Social structures not only are subject to change but create permanently and systematically some of the determinant forces of their change within themselves (p. viii).

This point of view is echoed in many of the social sciences; for example, anthropologist Francis Hsu quotes another anthropologist, Jules Henry:

> The late Jules Henry put it this way: "As I see it, the crucial difference between insect societies and human ones is that whereas the former are organized to achieve homeostasis, the organization of the latter seems always to guarantee and specifically provide for instability" (p. 465, Hsu; internal quote from Jules

Henry, "Homeostasis, Society and Evolution: A Critique," *Scientific Monthly*, 1955, LXXXI, p. 308).

We shall want to return to this kind of analysis, for it is basic to what we shall argue is a more truly social-psychological view of how man exists in society; both more conceptually coherent and more powerful as a tool for understanding either our social system in general or some particular part of it such as the educational system. But for the moment, so far as the evidence of different societies goes, one plausible argument is that any society generates some conformity and some nonconformity; and the questions would always have to be how much conformity and how much nonconformity, where it occurs, in what situations, for helpful or malevolent ends, etc.

This line of thought would lead one to try to (a) identify those aspects of the social structure which one wants to alter because they produce more conformity than seems desirable, and then (b) try to figure out how to alter them without altering other aspects of the structure which seem more benign (or less malign).

In a peculiar way, this analysis of the schools cuts two opposing ways. On the one hand, in criticizing our present educational system, it implies that changing it is a good idea. On the other hand, in implying that the educational system is only one facet of an evil social structure, it implies that criticizing the educational system alone is not of much use; the whole social structure must be reformed in order for any real good to result. The article does not state this clearly, but in a book which articulates a similar point of view, Michael Katz (in *Class, Bureaucracy, and Schools*) does make exactly this point: that criticism of the schools is somewhat beside the point, since school reform in and of itself will not change much at all. In his words,

... it is clear that the powers of schooling have been vastly overrated. Despite substantial financing and a captive audience, the schools have not been able to attain the goals set for them, with remarkably little change, for the last century and a quarter. They have been unable to do so because those goals have been impossible to fulfill. They require fundamental social reform, not the sort of tinkering that educational change has represented. If, by some miracle, the radical reformers were to capture the schools, and only the schools, for the next century, they would have no more success than educational reformers of the past (pp. 141-42).

Katz's book is a fascinating longer treatment of some of the same issues which we are considering with regard to the schools. His tone is more restrained than that of Lauter and Howe, and he seems more aware of the complexities of the problems raised in criticizing the schools (although this may be because he uses a whole book to make his argument, whereas Lauter and Howe had to compress their argument into a short article), but the underlying point of view seems roughly similar. As an example of the complexity of his consideration, look at his discussion of the relationship between education and poverty. Katz sees the same situation that Lauter and Howe see: "There is a pathetic lack of fit between the poor and the schools" (p. 139), but he also sees that "educational radicalism offers us as much an ideology as a solution" (p. 139). For, as he makes clear:

I suspect that what the poor want for their children is affluence, status, and a house in the suburbs rather than community, a guitar, and soul. They may prefer schools that teach their children to read and write rather than to feel and to be. If this is the case, then an uncomfortable piece of reality must be confronted. Educational radicalism is itself a species of class activity. It reflects an attempt at cultural imposition fully as much as the traditional educational emphasis on competition, restraint, and orderliness, whose bourgeois bias radicals are quick to excoriate... (p. 139).

Thus Katz sees the ideological nature of the radical criticism of schools as clearly as he sees the damage done by schools to many children, especially poor children.

(2) Do Lauter and Howe provide an understanding of the process of change? Underlying the criticism of the schools we have been considering is, as we said earlier, a thread of optimism: the assumption is that change of the schools and a corresponding change of an important segment of social reality is possible. One of the weaknesses of much radical criticism is that the process of change is left unexplored. How does change occur? What kinds of changes are possible? These are questions which a soundly based social-psychological conceptual analysis will have to face. Let us open a consideration of this question by considering the thought of Paolo Freire. To some extent, Freire is talking about the same topic as Lauter and Howe; but his tone is utterly different. He clearly is as interested in action to change things as he is in the effort to express his dissatisfaction with things; and, most important, he clearly recognizes the complexity of true change, radical change:

> The central problem is this: How can the oppressed, as divided, unauthentic beings, participate in developing the pedagogy of their liberation? Only as they discover themselves to be "hosts" of the oppressor can they contribute to the midwifery of their liberating pedagogy. As long as they live in the duality in which to be is to be like, and to be like is to be like the oppressor, this contribution is impossible. The pedagogy of the oppressed is an instrument for their critical discovery that both they and their oppressors are manifestations of dehumanization (Freire, p. 33).

Many interesting problems raised by Freire's general position we shall consider more fully later in discussing the work of Laing. For the moment, let us look at his clear recognition, both in this passage and throughout the rest of the book from which it is taken (*Pedagogy of the Oppressed*), that oppressed people cannot easily make a new society once they have overthrown their oppressors. Freire sees the problem as involving the image of man which people have. In an oppressive society, he assumes that everyone's image of man is molded by the oppressive reality, so that everyone has the same kind of image of what is desirable; the oppressed people, if freed, would try to be like the oppressors, since that is their only notion of how to be, and nothing much would be gained from Freire's point of view. The oppressed would be freer, to be sure, but they in turn would oppress others, so on balance, society would not be better off; the same oppressive social structures would continue to exist. This is one dilemma of any truly revolutionary ideology: how to make clear that real change is possible, given that the people promoting the change have been raised in the old order and thus, necessarily, have been formed at least to some extent by the malign forces which permeate the old order.

Thus here is someone considering the difficulties of change. Later in this book I shall explore that argument in more detail, and we will also explore opposing strands of thought of the sort we referred to already, which point out the inevitability of both nonconformity on the individual level and social conflict on the societal level. Both nonconformity and conflict prepare the way for change of some kind.

(3) What kind of evidence can be brought to bear on the Lauter and Howe theory? There is a heads-I-win-tails-you-lose aspect to their argument which is distressing, again not because it is theirs, but because it appears so often in respectable radical criticism. For example, they argue in this article that the high schools are evil because they train children for college, for such training is merely grooming faceless monsters of conformity who will help support the system. However, at the same time, the high schools are maligned for not training some children for college (the lower-class children). The underlying assumption behind this kind of argument is, perhaps, that the whole system is evil. That is, the analysis is no longer of a specific social institution, but of an entire society. Evil is seen as so per-

vasive that the attack is directed against everything which
exists. This aspect of their argument also shows very clear
affinities with Marcuse's thought as I shall show later.

(4) What alternatives do the authors propose? In attack-
ing all of present society, their view seems to restrict the
good to that which does not exist. Or, if this is not a correct
interpretation of their argument, then one can certainly say
that they leave the good society, the healthy, helpful
beneficial social institution, vague and unspecified. In short,
they propose no alternatives, save the vague one already
mentioned, when they ask for a social system which will
help children fulfill their own needs. Does the authors'
theoretical structure prevent them from suggesting any
plausible alternatives to the bad situation they are dissecting? Perhaps once one conceptually separates individual
from society—as they have in their theory—and talks of
individuals who are pushed around by social forces, about
individuals whose own needs are frustrated by society, one
has closed off all avenues of thought which might lead to
the theoretical construction of a better society than the one
we now have. Here is what often appears to be the fundamental weakness of American social criticism: it rides on the
easy separation of individual and society, on the necessity of
providing freedom for the individual, on the importance of
fulfilling one's own needs, and therefore it neglects terribly
the kind of thought which might lead to the creation of an
understanding of how people are related to society.

OVERVIEW

We have been examining a critical analysis of our
educational system which often extends to constitute a
critical analysis of our entire society. This analysis argues
that schools do not eliminate poverty and do not intend to
do so; in fact, they intend to maintain the status quo. They
are enemies of change because a certain group of people
benefits from this situation and has enough power to prevent others from changing the system. The people who
suffer from the system are first, those who are poor and

oppressed; and second, all those who are involved in the system, which frustrates everyone's true needs.

There are inadequacies in this analysis. One form of inadequacy is inconsistency: different parts of the argument do not fit together. Another difficulty is that as a conceptual structure it is well suited to describing a static society, but not at all suited to explaining change either in the past or in the future. Since change is not a process this theory can readily explain, it does not point toward any alternative which might replace the present situation.

Now we must begin to construct a position from which we can better comprehend the kind of relation which really exists between people and their society. The dominant image of this relation presented in the analysis just considered is that of oppression, although the question of who is the oppressor is not satisfactorily resolved. Can we find an image—embedded in a theory, a conceptual structure—which will provide a more coherent picture of the relation between people and society? Earlier I referred to Dahrendorf's analysis of society as inevitably made up of conflict; and of change as possibly arriving—at least partially—out of this conflict. I also referred to Freire's analysis of oppression as existing within people's minds as well as between individuals and social structures. These are both points which help us construct a truly social-psychological portrait of people in society. Let us continue to explore in this direction, beginning with the work of two very different writers, Herbert Marcuse and Carl Rogers. Each of these writers takes up, at some point, the issue of whether people have true needs of their own and how such needs might be gratified if they do exist.

First Marcuse, since his critical theory can be seen as underlying the kind of specific criticisms of our society I have just been discussing. After a look at Marcuse's thinking, with some particular attention to his analysis of the distinction between true and false needs, I shall turn to Carl Rogers, since he also considers the distinction between true and false needs, although he does not use these precise terms. He does, however, talk of the importance of people fulfilling their own needs, and we shall want to examine this line of thought carefully, since it also underlies some of the critical analysis just discussed. In this respect, the ideas of both Marcuse and Rogers are vital to the kind of critical analysis we have been considering. This is not to say that they have necessarily been a direct influence on contemporary critical writers, but only that they have each helped articulate a framework within which certain forms of criticism become not only possible, but conventional.

CHAPTER 3

Marcuse:
The Unhappy Consciousness

In my discussion of Marcuse, I shall be looking both forward and backward; that is, attempting to show how Marcuse's thought provides one kind of underpinning for such critical analyses of our society as we have just considered, and trying to show how his thought points us forward in the direction of our goal, the construction of a more systematic and adequate social psychological theory. I shall proceed by first describing some of the main themes of Marcuse's thought relevant to this book. After characterizing the main themes of importance to us here, I shall try to show how these themes are important.

MARCUSE'S THOUGHT

1. Marcuse's critical stance. The most general characterization one can offer of Marcuse's thought is that it is critical. Marcuse's thought arises from his vivid sense of our society as permeated by great danger, ugliness, suffering, and destruction. Anyone who does not have such a sense of our society is going to find Marcuse's writings somewhat opaque; not sharing Marcuse's central concern means that one will find Marcuse's writings incoherent, lacking any central unifying point. For Marcuse does not try to persuade the reader of the ugliness and pain of our society; he simply takes that for granted; and when he does rarely refer to "evidence" of our present state he does so in such an offhand manner that no one who did not originally agree with him would be persuaded to change his mind. For example: "Perhaps the most telling evidence (of how badly off we are) can be obtained by simply looking at television or listening to the AM radio for one consecutive hour for a couple of days, not shutting off the commercials, and now and then switching the station" (ODM, p. xvii). [1] Here his revulsion with the advertising and programming on the radio is so overwhelming that he assumes it is shared by all. This attitude toward our society is common enough; for example, it permeates Philip Slater's well-known book, *The Pursuit of Loneliness*. Slater is somewhat more concrete than Marcuse, but the tone is similar:

> Reentering America, one is struck first of all by the grim monotony of American facial expression—hard, surly, and bitter—and by the aura of deprivation that informs them. One goes abroad forewarned against exploitation by grasping foreigners, but nothing is done to prepare the returning traveller for the fanatical acquisitiveness of his compatriots. It is difficult to become reaccustomed to seeing people already weighted down with possessions acting as if every object they did not own were bread withheld from a hungry mouth.
>
> These perceptions are heightened by the contrast between the sullen faces of real people and the vision of happiness television offers: men and women ecstatically engaged in stereotyped symbols of fun—roaming through fields, strolling on beaches, dancing and singing. Smiling faces with chronically open mouths express their gratification with the manifold bounties offered by the culture (Slater, pp. xii-xiii).

1. ODM: *One-Dimensional Man*. Similarly I shall use initials to refer to other of Marcuse's writings later in the chapter, identifying them as I use them.

Slater looks around him and sees unhappy people; similarly, Marcuse looks around and hears ugly trash on the radio; and both men have made such perceptions of ugliness (and other related perceptions of suffering and destruction) central. And of course the Lauter and Howe article we have just been considering is permeated by a similar sense of present ills. I am not going to argue whether we are all so badly off as they think. But if one is to understand Marcuse's writings, a similar sense of crisis is a great help; and if one is not at least open to the possibility that our society is in serious trouble, then most of what Marcuse says is going to seem pointless. For those who do have a large and vivid sense of the suffering in our society, Marcuse seems extremely attractive.

2. *Marcuse's emphasis on ideas.* Marcuse differs from most social-psychologists in that he is massively nonempirical: he does not show clearly the facts on which his thinking is based. Thus, to follow his thought, we need more than sympathy with his critical stance. Oscar Wilde said, "It is much more easy to have sympathy with suffering than to have sympathy with thought" (in his essay "The Soul of Man under Socialism," in Ellman's collection, p. 255); yet what one needs above all to follow Marcuse's line of thought is a profound "sympathy with thought."

One of the most striking features of Marcuse's thought is his interest in the free play of ideas. He is fascinated by conceptual structures of thought and by the play of ideas through history; and although he professes to be interested in the ways in which ideas affect historical processes, he seems for the most part to assume that ideas and historical processes are just two aspects of the same sphere of reality. Thus he never stops to consider the empirical reality of the world in any concrete sense (although he refers to the world around us often enough) because he seems to think that his grasp of the ideas that animate that world suffices. He needs no data or statistical tables, no empirical material, because his ideas are (in his view) clear and adequate, and he writes as though talking about ideas is the same as talking about empirical reality. The conventional distinction between data and theory would strike him as bizarre. He is basically indifferent to the world of facts in the mundane sense in which the term *facts* is used by social scientists.

What further complicates his analyses is that future possibilities count for him as reality in the same sense that present facts do. They are described as contained within the present reality, and much of his writing can be seen as an attempt to show how one or another possibility is in the process of either being realized (brought to fruition) as in *Eros and Civilization,* or being stymied as in *One-Dimensional Man.*

For one example of how freely and easily Marcuse moves back and forth between the world of ideas and the world of empirical reality,[2] let us examine one part of his analysis of the domination which in his view permeates our society. He is talking (E&C, pp. 90-92 ff.) [3] about Freud's explanation of the need for instinctual repression as deriving from a scarcity of material goods. Then he says that this rationale for repression no longer makes sense: "The excuse of scarcity, which has justified institutionalized repression since its inception, weakens as man's knowledge and control over nature enhances the means for fulfilling human needs with a minimum of toil" (E&C, p. 92). The term *repression* is not of course being used in the strictly Freudian sense; as he points out in his Introduction, it is used "to designate both conscious and unconscious, external and internal processes of restraint, constraint, and suppression" (E&C, p. 8). Then he argues that because scarcity is no longer such a prominent fact (characteristically he does not fret about having to justify this claim; he just assumes that as he says it, you will believe it), that change should occur. There should be a "qualitative change in human needs" and there should occur a "development of needs beyond the realm of necessity" (E&C, p. 93). Then he argues that (a) this change is occurring; (b) this change should be occurring; and (c) the

2. I use this term knowing full well that Marcuse would not countenance the distinction I am making, as I have just made clear; but for want of any better way to discuss the matter, I shall use the conventional terms.

3. E&C: *Eros and Civilization.*

reasons this change is not occurring more rapidly are numerous. His later book, *One-Dimensional Man*, largely discusses why this change which he had been looking for has not occurred; and the still-later *An Essay on Liberation* is concerned with showing how it may be occurring after all.

Notice the way Marcuse jumps back and forth between ideas which are used as explanations for certain phenomena, and the phenomena themselves. He implies that when an *idea* that accounts for a *dynamic process* becomes outmoded, then that dynamic process has altered. And this conviction is basic to his thought, for his thought always has its eye on the future, as it were, and also revolves around the interpenetration of ideas about what ought to be and analyses of what is. A cogent summary of part of this aspect of Marcuse's thinking is offered by Shierry Weber in her essay "Individuation as Praxis":

> Traditionally, Marxism conceives a dialectical relationship between theory and praxis: theory is not disinterested but interested; it examines the present situation from the standpoint of a goal to be realized; it looks for tendencies in the present which, if realized, would lead beyond the present toward the goal. However, the goal, being something aimed at rather than something already existing, is an idea in the sense in which the German idealists used the word—an ideal conception. For Marxian socialism this idea has been the nature of man (Weber, pp. 22-23).

Clearly Marcuse is most interested in the realization of the idea of man; with this as his goal, he examines contemporary realities in order to see how they are helping or hindering this developing realization.

Marcuse is not so concerned as ordinary social scientists with accounting for present realities. If he had been, he would simply have argued (referring now to his argument that Freud's use of scarcity as an explanation for the existence of repression is outmoded): here we have a phenomenon (repression, and lack of human satisfaction); it might be occurring for any of the following reasons; now let us gather evidence which will support (or fail to support) each of the reasons. Instead he says: here we have a man (Freud) with a compelling theory; his theory used to be correct; now it is not correct; and therefore the world is or should be changing.

In discussing Marcuse's emphasis on ideas, I have mentioned two important features of the substance of his thought, which I shall return to, and whose importance should be emphasized now. First, his thought always has its eye on the future; he is concerned with diagnosing how present forces and dynamics of change are pushing us into a particular type of future existence. Second, he is interested in our idea of man and how we go about realizing that idea, how we go about changing ourselves so that we more closely resemble our image of what man should really be.

3. *Marcuse's interest in a better world.* The heart of Marcuse's thinking is his attempt to envision a way of living which would prove more favorable to "the free development of human needs and faculties" (ODM, p. ix) than our present way. Part of his attempt, to be sure, involves showing how our present society is destructive, how it causes needless suffering, how it distorts human nature. But his attacks on our society should be seen as deriving from his main focus, which is to persuade us that a better mode of life is possible and to hint about the directions in which we might search for such a better mode of life. Marcuse is unashamedly interested in a better world, in transcendence, as he would say, and he straightforwardly assumes that man is capable of making such a better world.

However, following Marcuse's thinking about this better world demands profound sympathy with thought, and Marcuse is about as far from those who claim to have simple answers to correct the problems of our world as can be imagined. Thus it is truly bizarre to see him being taken up by people who appear to believe in simple answers; there is nothing simple about Marcuse's approach. Lionel Trilling discusses Matthew Arnold in the following passage, but what he says seems pertinent to the current following Marcuse has acquired:

> A writer's reputation often reaches a point in its career where what he actually said is falsified even when he is correctly quoted. Such falsification—we might more charitably call it mythopoeia—is very likely the result of some single aspect of a man's work serving as a convenient symbol of what other people want to think (Trilling, *Matthew Arnold*, p. 9).

Marcuse essentially recommends hard thinking, rather than simple action, although of course he would not countenance any such distinction between thought and action. Thought and action in his view go together (in fact, at times he seems to imply that thought is indeed the highest form of action). But his books are noteworthy for their reliance on abstract thought and for the almost total absence of concrete suggestions for action; and when Marcuse does discuss concrete revolutionary actions (actions designed to help change the world) he is as likely to point out their shortcomings, their propensity to degenerate into mere outward gesture, as he is to applaud them.

The combination of his fiercely critical stance vis-à-vis our present society, and his interest in helping make a better world, have helped to make him a symbol for some of those who desire radical—even revolutionary—change. There is no question that Marcuse wants revolutionary change: he hopes for massive changes in the way we live and the way we are. But his fundamental focus is intellectual, not practical (to use a simpleminded distinction that he would not use himself). His writing is on the plane of rather abstract ideas, not on the plane of concrete suggestions for making a revolution.

4. *What kind of better world does Marcuse envision?* Let us attempt to penetrate some of what Marcuse actually says, rather than continuing with general characterization of his thought. The best place to look for a concise descrip-

tion of the better world he hopes we will move towards is in the concluding chapters of *Eros and Civilization.*

Here Marcuse tries to describe what a better world would look like. The title under which these chapters are gathered (Part II of *Eros and Civilization*) is "beyond the Reality Principle," which suggests that he is looking beyond our present world for something which does not yet exist, although the pertinent ideas exist, and he thinks there are some tendencies leading us all in their general direction.

In Chapter 7, he speaks in praise of fantasy which "remains free from the control of the reality principle . . . " (E&C, p. 141). Fantasy is good because it "has a truth-value of its own—namely, the surmounting of antagonistic human reality. Imagination envisions the reconcilization with the whole, of desire with realization, of happiness with reason" (p. 143). Fantasy involves keeping faith with "real possibilities" (p. 150) such as "the construction of a non-repressive instinctual development" (p. 150).

In Chapter 8, Marcuse begins talking about constructing an image of a "different reality" (p. 162). In this chapter, he makes very clear that when he talks about creating a new reality he is not talking about little rearrangements of the economic order; he is not talking about the workers assuming control of the means of production; he is not talking about distributing the wealth and ending war and such. He is talking about big changes: "The song of Orpheus pacifies the animal world, reconciles the lion with the lamb and the lion with man. The world of nature is a world of oppression, cruelty, and pain, as is the human world; like the latter, it awaits its liberation. This liberation is the work of Eros" (p. 166). And in Chapter 9, he says:

> Man is free only where he is free from constraint, external and internal, physical and moral—when he is constrained neither by law nor by need. But such constraint *is* the reality. Freedom is thus, in a strict sense, freedom from the established reality; man is free when the "reality loses its seriousness" and when its necessity

"becomes light" (leicht) (p. 187. Internal quotes are from Schiller, *Aesthetic Letters*).

Marcuse continues in the same vein, quoting again from Schiller:

> ... the need for and attachment to the real are "merely the results of want." In contrast, "indifference to reality" and interest in "show" (dis-play, Schein) are the tokens of freedom from work and a "true enlargement of humanity." In a genuinely humane civilization, the human existence will be play rather than toil, and man will live in display rather than need.
>
> These ideas represent one of the most advanced positions of thought. It must be understood that the liberation from the reality which is here envisaged is not transcendental, "inner," or merely intellectual freedom (as Schiller explicitly emphasizes) but freedom *in* the reality (p. 188. Internal quotes are from Schiller).

Clearly, in his own view, Marcuse is not abolishing the reality; as he says, he wants freedom *in* the reality. What he describes is a world where ordinary wants (for food, shelter, etc.) are taken care of, where people will live in a new manner characterized by beauty and play. He emphatically points out later that this is not possible in an otherwise repressive world; that is, for one person to live for beauty and in a spirit of play in an otherwise repressive world would not do at all. What he posits is an aesthetic function which governs "the entire human existence" (p. 188).

In Chapter 10, Marcuse states that there must be a transformation of libido (Freud's concept for sexual energy) corresponding to the transformation of societal institutions; his point seems to be that you cannot genuinely have the one without the other:

> ... the free development of transformed libido beyond the institutions of the performance principle differs essentially from the release of constrained sexuality within the dominion of these institutions. The latter process explodes suppressed sexuality; the libido continues to bear the mark of suppression and manifests itself in the hideous forms so well known in the history of civilization.... In contrast, the free development of transformed libido within transformed institutions, while eroticizing previously tabooed zones, time, and relations, would minimize the manifestations of mere sexuality by integrating them into a far larger order, including the order of work. In this context, sexuality tends to its own sublimation; the libido would not simply reactivate pre-civilized and infantile states, but would also transform the perverted content of these states (p. 202).

Here Marcuse describes the Freudian ideas of normal adult genital sexuality developing out of and through an integration of a series of infantile (pregenital) sexual stages. When these infantile stages (orality, anality, etc.) are not integrated, then (Freud thought) perversions and neurosis result. Marcuse states that he envisions not just a regression to these earlier sexual stages, and not an expression of sexual desires within our present oppressive reality, but rather a transformation of libido into Eros which would infuse all our living, work and play alike (so that work would, as he said earlier, be transformed into play).

Finally, in Chapter 11, Marcuse speaks of death: "The brute fact of death denies once and for all the reality of a non-repressive existence" he argues; and "The mere anticipation of the inevitable end, present in every instant, introduces a repressive element into all libidinal relations and renders pleasure itself painful" (p. 231). But no, he argues; death and time can also be done away with, or, at least, our awareness of them can be minimized. Here he seems to argue that in a world where all is pleasurable and joyful, time and death will cease to have the sigificance they now have; thus their bad effects will be avoided.

When the content of the passages we have excerpted is examined carefully, we see that realizing such a world as Marcuse envisions is not an easy task. One cannot simply depose the current rulers, whoever they may be, and expect such a new world to come into being. Something vastly more than a political revolution is required if Marcuse's ideas are to be realized and become the characteristics of the real world in which we all live. And that, clearly, is Marcuse's desire.

5. *How does change occur? Through transcendence and false consciousness.* Much of Marcuse's writing attempts to begin the process of change which will lead us to a better world, and two key phrases for this aspect of his thought are *transcendence* and *false consciousness.* He thinks change occurs when people can break through false consciousness and transcend the present reality. Let us try to explain these terms.

About *transcendence,* Marcuse says: "The terms 'transcend' and 'transcendence' are used throughout in the empirical, critical sense: they designate tendencies in theory and practice which, in a given society, 'overshoot' the established universe of discourse and action towards its historical alternatives (real possibilities)" (ODM, p. xi, footnote). Thus any given society has an "established universe of discourse." Now there are "tendencies" in any society which overshoot the established universe of discourse, but what does "overshoot" mean? It must refer to going beyond what is normally taken for granted. Marcuse seeks to identify tendencies in our society which go beyond what is conventional.

Discerning such tendencies involves abstraction which is not metaphysical insofar as the tendencies discerned are actual tendencies. In his words:

Such abstraction which refuses to accept the given universe of facts as the final context of validation, such "transcending" analysis of the facts in the light of their arrested and denied possibilities, pertains to the very structure of social theory. It is opposed to all metaphysics by virtue of the rigorously historical character of the transcendence. The "possibilities" must be within the reach of the respective society; they must be definable goals of practice. By the same token, the abstraction from the established institutions must be expressive of an actual tendency—that is, their transformation must be the real need of the underlying population. (ODM, p. xi)

Thus Marcuse talks of transcendence which is rigorously historical and not metaphysical, which refuses to accept the given universe of facts and yet must refer to a transformation which must be the real need of the underlying population.

Here is Marcuse again, talking about false consciousness this time. "Thus the break through false consciousness may provide the Archimedean point for a larger emancipation —at an infinitesimally small spot, to be sure, but it is on the enlargement of such small spots that the chance of change depends." (RT, p. 111) [4] He wants people to break through false consciousness; another word he uses in this context is *autonomous,* which describes the way people should be. How can people break through false consciousness and become autonomous? Marcuse says that for people

to become autonomous, to find by themselves what is true and what is false for men in the existing society, they would have to be freed from the prevailing indoctrination (which is no longer recognized as indoctrination). But this means that the trend would have to be reversed: they would have to get information slanted in the opposite direction. For the facts are never given immediately and never accessible imme-

4. RT: "Repressive Tolerance," an essay in Wolff, Moore, and Marcuse: *A Critique of Pure Tolerance.*

diately; they are established, "mediated" by those who made them; the truth, "the whole truth" surpasses these facts and requires the rupture with their appearance. This rupture—prerequisite and token of all freedom of thought and of speech—cannot be accomplished within the established framework of abstract tolerance and spurious objectivity because these are precisely the factors which precondition the mind *against* the rupture (RT, pp. 98-99).

Becoming autonomous requires breaking through false consciousness; but in a world where everything is subordinated to false consciousness and to indoctrination and distortion, in a one-dimensional world, as he has it in his well-known book of that title, there is precious little room for establishing a basis from which a larger emancipation might arise. Here we encounter an idea we have already met in an earlier discussion of the thinking of Paolo Freire (see pp. 52-53 above). Some aspects of Marcuse's thinking are very similar indeed to Freire's ideas.

The emancipation Marcuse is interested in is spiritual, or mental, or psychological first and primarily,[5] and only secondarily economic and political; in spite of his efforts to argue that the political realm has absorbed the psychological realm,[6] he writes as though the psychological realm is primary. Primary, that is, in the sense of being of critical and essential importance. This is evident in the long excerpt just quoted, where Marcuse talks not about throwing off the chains of economic and political oppression, but rather about a *rupture* with the *appearance* of things. Another word for what is required here is *transcendence*.

5. For example, Marcuse refers to "the sublimated realm of the soul or the spirit or the inner man" (ODM, p. 58).

6. Marcuse argues that "psychological categories" have "become political categories." His notion is that "our era tends to be totalitarian even where it has not produced totalitarian states" and thus since "the individual has neither the ability nor the possibility to be for himself, the terms of psychology become the terms of the societal forces which define the psyche" (*Eros and Civilization*, p. xi.).

Marcuse seems fundamentally interested in overcoming false consciousness by means of transcendence of the world of actual fact, and his effort at critical analysis of our society (as reflected in his published writings) would appear to be one manifestation of such a transcendence. The work of other critical thinkers would also fall into this category, as well as the spheres of art and philosophy in general (although not entirely). For Marcuse does have a real affection for the world of culture, which he would differentiate from that of society by arguing that culture embodies tendencies which work against—are subversive in—the society. In short, he has a romantic view of art and thought; by his definition, art is subversive. This does not mean necessarily that he would prefer what art and literary historians call romantic art to what is often called classical art. Not at all. For in his view, *all art* tends to erect a world of discourse which *stands opposed* to the conventional social world by epitomizing such values as beauty, which ordinarily take second place to such values as efficiency, practicality, and rationality. Thus, in Marcuse's view, anyone who acts as though beauty is more important than money would be subverting the conventional reality and helping to throw off false consciousness.

One of the central arguments in Marcuse's *One Dimensional Man* is that in contemporary society, " ... the progress of technological rationality is liquidating the oppositional and transcending elements in the 'higher culture' " (ODM, p. 56). He continues:

> Today's novel feature is the flattening out of the antagonism between culture and social reality through the obliteration of the oppositional, alien, and transcendent elements in the higher culture by virtue of which it constituted *another dimension* of reality (ODM, p. 5).

This other dimension has its own values (such as beauty, wholeness, and play as he makes clear in the later chapters of *Eros and Civilization*), which now have been incorporated into the established order and in fact now even serve "as instruments of social cohesion" (ODM, p. 57). Sometimes Marcuse argues that such values as "the sorrows and joys of the individual" and "the fulfillment of the personality" as used to inhere in this other dimension have now disappeared utterly; at other times he argues that they still exist, but their nature has changed insofar as they are tolerated. The fact that individual fulfillment is tolerated and even advertised as important (ODM, p. 56), the fact that it does not lead to radical change in the society, seems to Marcuse to mean that it is no longer what it used to be; its nature has altered. Marcuse would say that the meaning of these terms (individual, personality) has altered, and therefore they themselves have changed.

One of the functions of art and literature used to be that they created images of disruptive characters who do not sustain the social order, but in fact work against it, such characters as "the artist, the prostitute, the adulteress, the great criminal and outcast, the warrior, the rebel-poet, the devil, the fool" (ODM, p. 59). Marcuse argues that these characters have been transformed into "the vamp, the gangster, the star, the charismatic tycoon," types who "are no longer images of another way of life but rather freaks or types of the same life, serving as an affirmation rather than negation of the established order" (ODM, p. 59). Marcuse himself has an image of an earlier world where things were better than they are now, and he is intent on the necessity of replacing our present world with a new and better one. For one image of the earlier better world, he offers the following:

A backward, pre-technological world, a world with the good conscience of inequality and toil, in which labor was still a fated misfortune, but a world in which man and nature were not yet organized as things and instrumentalities. With its code of forms and manners, with the style and vocabulary of its literature and philosophy, this past culture expressed the rhythm and content of a universe in which valleys and forests,

villages and inns, nobles and villains, salons and courts
were a part of the experienced reality. In the verse and
prose of this pre-technological culture is the rhythm of
those who wander or ride in carriages, who have the
time and the pleasure to think, contemplate, feel and
narrate (ODM, p. 59).

He clearly sees a past world which, for all its faults, had
definite advantages over the one we now inhabit. One of its
advantages seems to be that it made transcendence easier
than it is now.

In Marcuse's view, transcendence and overcoming false
consciousness apparently require strenuous activity, but activity that is characteristically less bound up with guns and
the conventional ideas of revolution-cum-violence, and
more bound up with hard thought, mulling things over,
expanding one's consciousness or raising it, in today's catch
phrase. And, in fact, those young people who have taken
Marcuse most seriously (who have read him and thought
about what he has to say), those represented in the Breines
collection of essays, for example,[7] seem headed in this direction. They are "changing their own heads" and their own
way of living as best they can; they are characteristically not
engaged in organized group centered efforts to change our
society in the way that groups like SDS have tried to do.
They are not into confrontations with the establishment, in
the conventional senses, although they might well consider
themselves as revolutionary in intent (just as Marcuse
would argue that he is revolutionary in the true sense).

Some of the essays in the Breines book are worth drawing
attention to since they express what seems to me a natural
outgrowth of truly serious reflection on what Marcuse has
to say. One of the essays, taking very seriously Marcuse's
portrait of our one-dimensional society in which everything
partakes of domination, argues that "the people's language

7. Paul Breines edited *Critical Interruptions: New Left Perspectives
on Herbert Marcuse*. The book contains six essays, one each by Paul
Breines, Shierry Weber, Russell Jacoby, William Leiss, John David
Ober, and Jeremy Shapiro (New York: Herder & Herder, 1970).

is the language of domination" and talks of how obscurity is "a mark of truth in a world where clarity is a lie" (Jacoby, pp. 62-63). One logical outcome of reading Marcuse might then be silence, or complete withdrawal from the world, as in suicide, if one takes very seriously his idea that our society is one-dimensional. That is, part of Marcuse's thought makes clear that negations of the surrounding reality, of the sort involved in true transcendence, are not easily come by; thus complete silence or suicide, by their extremity, can be seen as fitting in the light of the more pessimistic quality of some of Marcuse's writings.

However, Marcuse wavers between pessimism and optimism; and if his pessimism finds expression in his conviction that our society is completely oppressive, his optimism finds expression in his analyses of trends in our society which provide grounds for hope that some real change is indeed possible. Thus, in another essay in this volume, "Individuation as Praxis," Shierry Weber discusses individuation as one way of overthrowing false consciousness and negating the surrounding oppressive reality. The term *individuation* is taken from Jung, but in using it Weber is being faithful to that part of Marcuse which deplores the submergence of individual people in our mass society. In her view, individuation, or realizing the individual is not merely a personal project but a political one as well; as she says, "personal experience is by nature social" (p. 26),[8] and in a very clear sense, her essay flows from Marcuse's thinking as much as does Jacoby's praise of obscurity and even silence. Still other essays in this volume undertake to extend some of Marcuse's ideas or to explore them in some depth. None of them cries for revolution with guns in the streets.

Thus Marcuse argues that change in our society depends on the individual's ability to shed false consciousness. This can be a revolutionary activity, but not in the image of Che Guevara or Fidel Castro. Now obviously—as we know well from our experience of the past several years—this kind of

8. This echoes Marcuse's praise of "Freud's individual psychology" as being "in its very essence social psychology" (*Eros and Civilization*, p. 16).

view can become watered down into a romanticism of the sort triumphantly thrust forward in Reich's *Greening of America*, or in Roszak's *The Making of a Counter Culture*. These authors argue that a real change is occurring, not by guns and a French or Russian revolution model, but via a different one; people are changing, mostly young ones now, but more and more people as time goes by. They make it too easy to be revolutionary, in this "shedding false consciousness" sense.

For example, they make it seem as though anyone who cooks on a wood stove, or who refuses to wear conventional clothing, or who collects unemployment insurance, or listens to loud rock music, is engaged in the process of revolutionary activity, overthrowing the present oppressive false consciousness. Marcuse makes wonderfully apparent that things are not so simple; the oppressive reality penetrates almost everywhere. Shierry Weber makes this rather clear in differentiating between abstract negation and determinate negation. What Roszak and Reich are talking about is all too often abstract negation: it is simply opposition to whatever is around. "Negative behavior and dress become a style; life becomes life-style. The external gesture is mistaken for the subjective experience," as Shierry Weber says (p. 40). And then she shows that the failure here in part is a "failure to understand the existing system as one of intentions, and destructive intentions, rather than institutions, behavior, or styles . . . " (p. 40).

Marcuse would surely agree with Weber here, for although in places Marcuse expresses some attraction to certain elements of the so-called counterculture, in other places his honesty leads him to insist that mere style and surface gesture are not enough. And what, for Marcuse, makes most of the counterculture mere gesture is its lack of connection with systematic thought, its failure to rise to the level of determinate negation (that which uses the "energy of negation for a process of counter-integration," Weber, p. 40).

To review briefly: I have pointed out that Marcuse is fundamentally a social critic who desires change in our present social and human reality. He is interested in providing us with ideas enabling us to transcend our present reality and to create a new and better one. He emphasizes considerably the importance of individual consciousness in this process of transcendence and overcoming false consciousness. In his view, such transcendence is difficult because the oppressive reality penetrates everywhere; we have difficulty in achieving radically new ideas since each of us is constrained, in very subtle ways, by the dominating influence of conventional reality. And the world he would like to see is radically different from our present world in ways that make it fundamentally difficult for us to imagine what this new life would be like.

Marcuse's social criticism can well be compared to that of Thomas Carlyle, the nineteenth-century writer-prophet. The prominent issue for both men is, in part, the condition of man: how is it altering or failing to alter; both are less interested in precise evaluation of various bodies of fact than in spiritual diagnosis. What is happening today in the most general sense. And Carlyle shares with Marcuse the same moral seriousness.

Marcuse's criticisms of our society are to some extent the usual ones (poverty, war, racism, conformity, advertising, ugliness) and to some extent unusual. The unusual component of his criticism is based on his strong feeling that what is possible is more important than what is actual: reality has two realms, that of possibility and that of actuality, and the former is more important than the latter. Since so much of his critical analysis of our society moves from his desire to make actual that which now is only possible—a world in which all is freedom and beauty, where necessity has receded to a dim vanishing point—his criticism loses touch with the concrete actualities of our society and often seems directed against all existing societies, against any society that ever has actually existed. Perhaps Marcuse would not agree with this, since he makes quite clear in *One-Dimensional Man* that he thinks the present-day American society is radically different from previous societies. But he provides little evidence to support this contention. Some of the evidence of the totalitarian one-dimensional nature of our present society he alludes to, is not clearly pertinent solely to our society. For example, he talks of alienating labor, but his is clearly an evil which has not arisen recently in our civilization.

Although it is hazardous to identify those aspects of our present society which Marcuse thinks make it uniquely evil, perhaps it is our affluence and material well-being which Marcuse finds our gravest fault: that we have not used our affluence better, to free more men from unsatisfying labor, to enable more men to rise above the level of mere existence.

CRITICAL EVALUATION OF MARCUSE'S THOUGHT

As long as one stays at this abstract level, Marcuse is surely correct in his critical evaluation of our social state. As long as one simply says, "Look at how wealthy our country is; why are not more people happy?" then one must agree with Marcuse that something is dreadfully wrong. But as soon as Marcuse gets down to the specifics of the indictment, one has trouble following his argument.

For example, one of Marcuse's major arguments against our society is that it promotes systematic confusion between true and false needs. He sees the advertising industry as the paradigm of this confusion, in that advertisements often try to create needs in people.

This distinction between false and true needs is vital to Marcuse's view of our society, and by examining it we can see that Marcuse is indicting not just our society (with its perhaps uniquely developed advertising apparatus) but all societies. Marcuse says that false needs

> are those which are superimposed upon the individual by particular social interests in his repression: the needs which perpetuate toil, aggressiveness, misery, and injustice. Their satisfaction might be most gratifying to the individual, but this happiness is not a condition which has to be maintained and protected if

it serves to arrest the development of the ability (his own and others) to recognize the disease of the whole and grasp the chances of curing the disease (ODM, p. 5).

What is interesting is his admission that satisfaction of false needs may be gratifying to the individual; in a sense, he is impugning the capacity of the individual to judge what is truly good for him. Marcuse goes on to clarify this: "In the last analysis, the question of what are true and false needs must be answered by the individuals themselves, but only in the last analysis; that is, if and when they are free to give their own answer" (ODM, p. 6). Thus he backs away from declaring that any "tribunal" (p. 6) can decide what needs are true and ought to be satisfied; but he also argues that individuals in our present society are not truly free and autonomous, and therefore are not capable of knowing their own true needs. At this point one asks whether Marcuse conceives of any actual society as having been (or being) populated by free and autonomous people. He might argue that our society used to have more such men; but he would always insist that no society makes freedom and autonomy easy, and thus we need a new society.

At this very abstract level, it is easy to follow the argument. But if one starts to wonder how we can tell true needs from false, how can we discern true needs within us, then one feels that Marcuse is not so much help after all. He gives no guidance. Whatever Marcuse's answer, it certainly has nothing to do with survey questionnaires and asking people what they need; nor does it have anything to do with psychological testing of the sort that projective tests accomplish. Marcuse may have a method for discerning real needs, but he fails to make clear what that method is.

Further, given his definition of a better world as one in which people live for beauty and play, it is not clear that men in any society have ever been given to gratifying their true needs (for beauty and play) in any widespread manner. But, by the same token, it is likely that our society has as many people living for aesthetic principles as any society ever has. Marcuse would see this kind of approach to his argument as silly and irrelevant because it is dragging his theoretical argument down to the level of actuality, and, as he repeats the whole point of critical theory such as his own is to show the defects in what is actual by comparing it to what is possible. And part of his animus against our society is that since the possibilities for freedom are greater (given his fundamental assumption that economic scarcity is no longer such a major problem), the fact that we do not now exist in freedom means that our society is worse than previous ones because, in his view, various forces (unidentified) are working hard to contain the possibilities inherent in our economic prosperity.

If Marcuse's criticisms of society pertain not just to our own society, then his arguments that our society is uniquely one-dimensional may not make sense. He argues that individual private consciousness is being swallowed in social public consciousness, which he reads as a kind of oppression. But he is not persuasive when he argues that this is a peculiarly twentieth-century or American phenomenon.

In Marcuse's earlier book, *Eros and Civilization,* he makes much clearer than in *One-Dimensional Man* that he is comparing all of social actuality with an ideal, and finding that actuality severely wanting. He is apparently attempting to establish "a conceptual basis outside the established system" (E&C, p. 6) and he makes clear that his notion of the established system is very broad indeed, coextensive in fact with what Freud called the reality principle. His notion is that there is a social dimension to the Freudian concept of the reality principle, and in order to clarify this, he refers to the form of the reality principle which is characteristic of our society as "the performance principle" (E&C, pp. 34-35). Two points are pertinent here: first, that he does not carefully establish exactly when this performance principle becomes important in our civilization, and at times he talks as though it has been the dominant characteristic of our society for centuries. Second, he often neglects to refer to the performance principle and, in fact, entitles the second half of this book "Beyond the Reality Principle," indicating that, in a very important sense, he is attempting to examine what we ordinarily think of as reality in the light of what is ideally possible.

Eros and Civilization shows that Marcuse is concerned not simply with a particular social organization like that of mid-twentieth-century America. Rather, he is concerned with civilization as a whole, and Freud's *Civilization and Its Discontents* is an important model for him. But in a very peculiar fashion, in spite of Marcuse's insistence on identifying the particular social provenance of any conceptual framework (illustrated, for example, in his attempt to show how Freud's ideas were related to Freud's social context), he himself characteristically attempts to erect a conceptual structure which will attain a clarity and truth somehow independent of any particular society. In this respect he is similar to Hegel, who also tried to how how conceptual structures are linked to social circumstances, and yet simultaneously tried to erect a conceptual structure which would represent a culmination of the preceding centuries of thought and attain a kind of transcendental truth. Similarly, Marcuse's ideal world (see the latter half of *Eros and Civilization*) is radically different not just from twentieth-century American society, but from societies in general. His vision is truly transcendental.

The problem with criticism such as Marcuse's is that it is perhaps too sweeping to have much impact on social scientists. When they are concerned with changing reality, they isolate a small segment of it to bear the brunt of the attack. But Marcuse certainly does have an impact on others, whose vision is more apocalyptic. Cannot at least some of his ideas be saved from the purveyors of apocalypse? For he has indeed a discerning grasp of important features of the relation between people and their society. But first let us continue with our critical evaluation of his thought.

That Marcuse considers himself a careful analyst of reality is clear from his remarks about Norman O. Brown, who has achieved some fame as an interpreter of Freud.[9] In a

9. See in particular Norman O. Brown, *Life Against Death* (New York: Random House, 1959).

discussion-review of *Love's Body* (a later work by Brown), Marcuse rebukes Brown, essentially for losing touch with reality. As Marcuse points out, "what we call reality, Brown calls illusion, lie, dream" ("Love Mystified," p. 228). And Marcuse goes on to state:

> Brown's concept of illusion (sleep, dream) covers, undifferentiated, the latent and the overt content of history, or, it de-realizes reality. To him, the political kingdoms are "shadows," political power is a fraud; the emperor has no new clothes, he has no clothes at all. But unfortunately, he does: they are visible and tangible; they make history. In terms of the latent content, the kingdoms of the earth may be shadows; but unfortunately, they move real men and things, they kill, they persist and prevail in the sunlight as well as in the dark of night. The king may be an erected penis, and his relation to the community may be intercourse; but unfortunately, it is also something very different and less pleasant and more real (*Negations*, p. 235).

Then he continues:

> The roots of repression are and remain real roots; consequently, their eradication remains a real and rational job. What is to be abolished is not the reality principle; not everything, but such particular things as business, politics, exploitation, poverty (pp. 235-36).

There is no question that Marcuse's points about Brown are well taken. Brown does float off into an ethereal world where it becomes very difficult to distinguish, in concrete terms, what he is talking about; he clearly disapproves of our present world, but what kind of world does he want to replace it?

But reading Marcuse can leave us with the same kind of feeling. Although Marcuse intends to describe reality, he seldom convinces the reader that he is in close touch with it; and so far as his vision of a better world goes, he floats off into the same nebulous world as Brown does: his ideas seem equally impractical. Of course, if we asked Marcuse whether his expectations for a better world where all is pleasure, where the lion and the lamb lie down together, are realistic, he would reply that our concepts of reality and of what is possible are distorted by our current social situation, which is oppressive in the extreme. He would add that the whole point of critical social thinking of the sort he is engaging in is to keep alive ideas which seem impracticable. Against these arguments there is perhaps no defense. But Brown as well could use the same argument. Marcuse rebukes Brown for wanting to abolish reality, but seems to say the same thing. Then who is Marcuse to call Brown unrealistic?

HOW MARCUSE CAN HELP US IN OUR QUEST FOR A TRUE SOCIAL PSYCHOLOGY

Authenticity.

An interesting perspective on Marcuse's thought is found in Lionel Trilling's recent book, *Sincerity and Authenticity*. Some brief review of Trilling's argument is necessary. Trilling discusses "the moral life in process of revising itself" in our culture (p. 1).[10] He believes that "sincerity" as a component of the moral life became important around the same time that individualism became an important aspect of Western culture; and he tries to link together the sudden efflorescence of the theater (p. 10), the conception of the villain (p. 14), the increase in the rate of social mobility (p. 15), the rise of the concept of society (p. 18), the decline of feudalism and the ever-increasing urbanization of the population (p. 20), and the impulse to write autobiography (p. 24). All of these occurred during roughly the same period, the late sixteenth and early seventeenth centuries (p. 19), and weaving all these occurrences together enables us to understand the rise of the conception of sincerity as a virtue. He also discusses the decline of the concept of sin-

10. Until otherwise indicated, the page references are to Trilling's *Sincerity and Authenticity* (Cambridge: Harvard University Press, 1972).

cerity (p. 5), and he argues that its place has been—or is being—taken by the idea of authenticity. As he says:

> The word "authenticity" comes so readily to the tongue these days and in so many connections that it may very well resist such efforts of definition as I shall later make, but I think that for the present I can rely on its suggesting a more strenuous moral experience than "sincerity" does, a more exigent conception of the self and of what being true to it consists in, a wider reference to the universe and man's place in it, and a less acceptant and genial view of the social circumstances of life. At the behest of the criterion of authenticity, much that was once thought to make up the very fabric of culture has come to seem of little account, mere fantasy or ritual, or downright falsification. Conversely, much that culture traditionally condemned and sought to exclude is accorded a considerable moral authority by reason of the authenticity claimed for it, for example, disorder, violence, unreason (p. 11).

Now we can see the relevance of Marcuse, for we might argue that one of the underlying conceptions animating his work is that of authenticity, in the sense in which Trilling defines it in the passage just quoted. Marcuse himself does use the term *authentic* occasionally to describe (favorably) the kind of personal existence he views as worthwhile. For example, in an interesting passage on the current shibboleth of self-actualization he points out that much of what passes for self-actualization,

> isolates the individual from the one dimension where he could "find himself": from his political existence, which is at the core of his entire existence. Instead, it encourages nonconformity and letting-go in ways which leave the real engines of repression in the society entirely intact, which even strengthen these engines by substituting the satisfactions of private and personal

rebellion for a *more than private* and personal, and therefore *more authentic,* opposition (my italics, *Repressive Tolerance,* pp. 114-15).

Marcuse views an authenticity which contains, in Trilling's words (p. 11), "a wider reference to the universe and man's place in it, and a less acceptant and genial view of the social circumstances of life."

Trilling makes much of Hegel's distinction between the "honest soul" and the "disintegrated consciousness," and he argues that this distinction and his own between sincerity and authenticity are parallel. What Hegel called *the honest soul* is what ordinarily we would call the *sincere* person: uncomplicated, direct, and consistent in his relations with things. And what Hegel called the *disintegrated consciousness* might correspond to what we call *authenticity.* Certainly Marcuse would find this reasonable, since he himself refers several times to the *unhappy consciousness* favorably, applauding the way in which unhappiness leads one to stand against the current reality, and deploring the extent to which the unhappy consciousness is no longer so typical of our society as it was fifty years ago (Chapter 3 of *One-Dimensional Man,* "The Conquest of the Unhappy Consciousness").

Trilling points up a contradiction between two ideas which are contained in the notion of authenticity: one, that a person is connected with a wider society; the other, that a person is disconnected from (contemptuous of) the surrounding society. This emerges in his discussion of Marcuse.

In his last chapter, Trilling discusses the popularity of the views of Ronald Laing.[11]

What Laing tells us about the mind in relation to society is of course not new in any essential way. It is a view to which in one degree of intensity or another, our culture has long been habituated. The inculpation

---

11. For example, *The Divided Self,* and especially *The Politics of Experience.*

of society has become with us virtually a category of thought. We understand a priori that the prescriptions of society pervert human existence and destroy its authenticity (p. 161).

Then he continues, saying that doubtless there will be

> . . . no ready disposition to accept a view of the mind in its relation to society which proposes the idea that authenticity is exactly the product of the prescriptions of society and depends upon these prescriptions being kept in force. Such a view has been advanced, and not by some conservative humanist but by a writer whose own inculpation of society is scarcely mild, by none other than Herbert Marcuse (p. 161).

What Trilling refers to here is not such passages as those already quoted from Marcuse (e.g., on page 82-3, above), where authentic opposition to society is glorified, but rather those parts of Marcuse's writings [12] where he deplores the decline of personal automony and the rise of masses in which each person has less personal living space and where "The mediation between the self and the other gives way to immediate identification" (OFC, p. 47).[13] Rather interestingly, what Marshall McLuhan waxes ecstatic over as the rise of the "global village," Marcuse deplores:

> The shrinking of the ego, its reduced resistance to others appears in the ways in which the ego holds itself constantly open to the messages imposed from outside. The antenna on every house, the transistor on every beach, the jukebox in every bar or restaurant are

12. Trilling cites *Eros and Civilization*, pp. 86-87; but the whole essay "The Obsolescence of the Freudian Concept of Man" is a more extended treatment of the same theme, and of course there are other places where Marcuse touches on these ideas.

13. OFC: "The Obsolescence of the Freudian Concept of Man," an essay in *Five Lectures* by Marcuse.

as many cries of desperation—not to be left alone, by
himself, not to be separated from the Big Ones
. . . (OFC, p. 49).

As Trilling points out, Marcuse is concerned with "the
devolution of the power of the superego, which he sees as
resulting in a deplorably lowered degree of individuality
and autonomy" (Trilling, p. 164). Marcuse thinks that the
Freudian concept of man is not so relevant now as it was
fifty years ago because the conditions of society have
changed. In Marcuse's words:

> The sweeping changes in advanced industrial society
> are accompanied by equally basic changes in the pri-
> mary mental structure. In the society at large, techni-
> cal progress and the global coexistence of opposed
> social systems lead to an obsolescence of the role and
> autonomy of the economic and political subject. The
> result is ego formation in and by masses, which depend
> on the objective, reified leadership of the technical
> and political administration. In the mental structure,
> this process is supported by the decline of the father
> image, the separation of the ego ideal from the ego and
> its transference to a collective ideal, and a mode of
> desublimation which intensifies social control of li-
> bidinal energy (OFC, p. 59).

Marcuse's argument seems to be that the old society
which Freud discussed led to the sort of individual repression which was not, in Marcuse's view, entirely beneficial.
But it also had its advantages: it formed some relatively
autonomous characters. Now we have a society (Marcuse
argues) where autonomy is more difficult than ever before.
Trilling argues that Marcuse prefers the old repressive
family upbringing which produced much pain and suffering
and some character, although Trilling may not be correct.
For Marcuse's true ideal is not any historical condition that
has ever existed, but one still in the future. The historical
condition Marcuse hopes for is one where true individuality

is possible, but in concert with others and without pain and suffering, without exigent reality.

And, interestingly, Marcuse seems to look to just that unhappy consciousness which Hegel and Trilling were discussing as the potential source of some truly progressive change in human existence. Marcuse claims that the unhappy consciousness has a catalytic force ("Repressive Tolerance," p. 115) which will help transform our present reality, and he praises alienation (p. 114) because it involves a turning against our present society.

Marcuse thinks of this unhappy consciousness as connected with culture (art, philosophy, critical social theory, etc.), and the disappearance of this unhappy consciousness (see *One-Dimensional Man*) distressed him. The more optimistic tone of his later writings is clearly attributable to the signs of unhappiness which, during the late sixties, were everywhere around us.

Along these lines, Marcuse has some praise for Freudian theory in his essay on its obsolescence, as when he says " ... psychoanalysis draws its strength from its obsolescence: from its insistence on individual needs and individual potentialities which have become outdated in the social and political development" (OFC, p. 60). Marcuse is clearly devoted to psychoanalytic theory, and although from any orthodox view Marcuse is playing games with Freudian terminology and concepts (to the point where one wonders whether he is trying to exemplify that spirit of play he so values), there is no question of his true devotion to some of the ideas of psychoanalysis. And one of the enigmas of Marcuse is his devotion to so much of our culture. He is steeped in Western philosophy (some of it, anyway) and art and ideas; he is in favor of individuality, which has for so long been one of the passwords of our civilization; and, although he never explains how, in a world where freedom and necessity coincide (and the lion and the lamb lie down together), we are simultaneously going to have art and philosophy and true individuality, nonetheless he thinks it possible.

Thus one of Marcuse's ideas which we will find useful is

that a better world can only come about if there are relatively autonomous individuals whose urges to transcend the
immediate world about them will be fired by an unhappy
consciousness produced by a conflict between themselves
and the society about them. Conflict—e.g. between culture
and society—is primary for Marcuse; and what he worries
most about (as in his *One-Dimensional Man*) is the possibility that all conflict will disappear, that individuals will be
swallowed up in a kind of mass man, that all contradiction
within society will be nullified and eliminated. Marcuse
does hint—as Trilling correctly points out—that the kind of
family structure which Freud was analyzing fifty years ago
or so might have been responsible for creating the kind of
autonomous men Marcuse values so highly, but this is only
a hint and is nowhere spelled out in Marcuse's thought. So
we shall not look in Marcuse's writings for any detailed
account of how individuality and autonomy are best fostered, but instead make careful note of the high estimation
he places on the presence of conflict in a society as an agency
of change. This issue has already been raised, in the discussion of our schools; Dahrendorf pointed out the importance
of societal conflict as a vehicle of societal change. And I
have already taken the point from Goffman (see Chapter 5)
about the way in which the self arises out of a process of
pushing off from or standing away from a surrounding social
reality.

How else can Marcuse help us? Most importantly, perhaps, by his strenuous concern with ideas; for however abstract his thought may appear at some points, he can help us
see the importance of taking ideas seriously. Social psychology can use a strong dose of his high regard for ideas and
theoretical effort. There is no other way for social-psychological theory to develop, except by respecting the particular intellectual demands of carefully working out ideas.

Finally, Marcuse's concern with change and with the
depiction of good society is important. The main thrust of
his thinking is that real change is difficult, that it requires
hard and careful thought. In these respects, Marcuse seems
far superior to most critics of our society; he sees far better

than most the difficulties of real change. What makes his views of change particularly worthwhile? He adds a psychological dimension to the sociological-economic-political one. Marcuse sees the importance of a change in the structure of consciousness, in the way we think and experience, which must accompany or even precede political and sociological changes if the world is to improve. And this is a point too often neglected by all but religious writers (whose influence so often fails to penetrate the realms of intellectual or political discourse).

CHAPTER 4:

Ronald Laing:
In Search of Autonomy

The ideal of personal autonomy underlies much of Marcuse's criticism of our society. Laing makes this ideal much more central: with him it is no longer an underlying component, but is one of the central features of the conceptual structure he attempts to erect.

Laing is a rather complicated writer; his many books do not fit neatly together. Here I shall try to disentangle his important themes, concentrating on the social-psychological dimension of his writing, particularly his views of the influence of the family on the individual, and the influences people have on one another in their daily interactions.

The main thread of our discussion of Laing's social psychology will be that he offers two points of view: he argues that social institutions (the family is his principal example, but he refers to society in general as well) corrode the self. His underlying assumption is that there is some way—not specified but implied throughout—for the self to get away from these corrosive effects. Going mad may be one way to get away; another might be to restructure the social institutions altogether so that they no longer have any bad effects on the self, on the people who inhabit the institutions.

Laing offers another point of view which does not fit very well with the first that the very structure of the self is constituted by the social institutions in which it is embedded. He makes this point in a variety of ways, arguing persuasively, for example, that in two-person interactions each person is inextricably bound up with (in) the other person, thus never really independent.

The point of emphasizing these two themes in Laing's writings is partly to draw attention to him as an original thinker whose main contributions lie not in his explorations of madness (which is of course what he is best known for), but in his analysis of the intricacies of involvement between self and other, between one person and other people; but principally, though, because I want to draw together ideas which will help us understand the general issues discussed earlier which arise out of contemporary social criticism. A brief way to state one of the central issues is to ask: is the self adversely affected by the surrounding social institutions; if so, can anything be done? Our focus throughout the following discussion of Laing as with Marcuse, should be both forward and backward; not so much centered in Laing and his thought as is in looking forward to a more viable social-psychological theory, and in looking backward to our earlier discussion of social criticism.

LAING'S THOUGHT

1. *Tone.* Laing's tone varies, from extreme anger at one end to a relatively dispassionate scientific objectivity at the other. He is better known for the anger, as exemplified in most of *The Politics of Experience*. As with Marcuse, this angry tone is connected with a point of view readily assimilated by those dissatisfied with one or another aspect of our present society. Thus Laing, like Marcuse, is important for some social critics. But the more dispassionate side of Laing's writing is less well known; most pronounced in his earlier writings, then missing for a while, it has reappeared recently. His first book, *The Divided Self* (1959), was an attempt to understand the experience of schizophrenics. The dispassionate tone prevailed in this work and well into the middle sixties. Then, with *The Politics of Experience* (1967), came the most vivid expression of his anger. In his

most recent talks and articles, however, the anger has diminished.

2. *Laing's conceptual ambitions.* Like Marcuse, Laing is important for us because he takes theoretical work seriously; in the introduction to the study of schizophrenic families (*Sanity, Madness and the Family,* which he wrote with Aaron Esterson), he elaborates a conceptual structure which places the behavior characteristic of schizophrenics in a familial context. He develops special theoretical terms, such as *nexus,* meaning the structure of the dynamics of the family, the way in which the family's interactions fit together. This term underscores the focus, which is not just on the behavior of individual persons, but on the behavior of persons-in-relation to one another. Laing and Esterson say:

> We are studying the persons who comprise this nexus, their relationships, and the nexus itself, in so far as it may have structures, processes, and effects as a system, not necessarily intended by its members, not necessarily predictable from a knowledge of its members studied out of context. (SMF, p. 21) [1]

Their interest is in the system, as well as in the individuals, and this is what makes their approach social-psychological.

In addition to the attempt in *Sanity, Madness and the Family* to describe the family system, the nexus within which individuals live, Laing also tries in other books (particularly *Self and Others, Interpersonal Perception,* and *The Politics of the Family*) to extend social psychology in other directions. In these books, the focus is on how the individual influences and is influenced by another person, and some of Laing's terms show his own particular way of understanding these influences. By *induction,* Laing means the way in which person A induces person B to change by telling B what he thinks B is or should be. Laing is concerned with subtle inductions conveyed nonverbally by tone of voice or expression, or conveyed subtly as a covert

1. SMF: *Sanity, Madness and the Family.*

element of a long, extended series of communications, as well as with the more overt inductions; as when a parent tells a child "You are no good" or when A tells B "you are mad." Laing sees such statements as attributions or, in his term, inductions.

Another of Laing's terms is *projection,* by which he means not the simple Freudian defense mechanism, but a way of working on someone else psychologically, trying to make him or her into something. So *projection* and *induction* seem to be different words for the same phenomenon, which Laing explores in a number of his books.

I shall return to these concepts in discussing the main substance of Laing's social-psychological ideas; but for the moment, my point is simply to present Laing's attempt to create a cogent social-psychological theory. In the most general sense, Laing tries to integrate Freudian ideas, emphasizing the social context within which people live and act. He uses the term *projection,* a conventional Freudian term confined to an internal psychological operation in which a person attributes his own feelings to another to avoid acknowledging that the feeling is his own; this may involve an overt action, an expression, or simply a thought. But then Laing emphasizes the overt component of the Freudian projection, especially the way in which the act affects the other person. Laing's focus, as he himself says, is on the *projected upon* person (PF, p. 83),[2] and on the process whereby one person affects another by projecting an image on him and inducing him to live out that image.

Both Marcuse and Laing have been greatly influenced by Freud, and both have tried to rework Freudian ideas to make them apply to social as well as intrapsychic processes. Further both have used Freudian ideas as a critical instrument to attack social institutions. Freud's ideas can lend themselves to critical attacks on society as well as to defense of existing institutions.

What are Laing's other intellectual debts? To other studies of family processes, perhaps; to phenomenological

2. *The Politics of the Family.*

philosophy, certainly; and to such existential philosophers as Sartre. This latter debt is most apparent when Laing tries to describe the existence—or the being, the experience—of a schizophrenic in *The Divided Self*. One of the central concepts in that book is *ontological insecurity*, a term clearly derived from existential philosophy. A very rough translation of this term is anxiety derived from not feeling at home in the world; probably *anxiety* is the everyday term most closely approximating Laing's phrase. Laing uses this term in an effort to clarify the peculiar nature of the schizophrenic's experience, arguing that the schizophrenic suffers from ontological insecurity; but clearly Laing shares with the existential philosophers a conviction that this kind of insecurity or anxiety is typical of all human beings. Thus this term illustrates a tendency which appears in even this earliest of Laing's books, to describe all human experience. Although his ostensible topic in this early book is schizophrenic experience, its application to the human condition is made explicit in the preface to the second edition of this book (*The Divided Self*).

3. *Laing's writing about the family.* Laing's views on the family and its influences on the individual are contained for the most part in two volumes, *The Politics of the Family*, and (co-authored with Aaron Esterson) *Sanity, Madness and the Family*. Another book, *The Politics of Experience*, refers to the effects of society on the individual and does so in ways which seem to imply that for Laing the family is often a representative social institution whose effects on the individual are paradigmatic of the effects of society. He offers no sustained argument to this effect, but to suppose that he thinks this does make sense of what he says, and enables the reader to see continuity among various of his writings.

Laing's interest in family dynamics seems to have arisen out of his clinical experience with psychotics, particularly schizophrenics. *Sanity, Madness and the Family* is an attempt to place the behavior characteristic of schizophrenics in an intelligible context (the family of the schizophrenic). Although most of the analysis in this book concentrates on showing how family processes influence the schizophrenic's behavior, Laing and Esterson focus not only on the person-in-the-family, but on the family dynamics themselves (the *nexus*, SMF, p. 26). Their truly social-psychological concern interpenetrates with their clinical concern; they want not merely to diagnose and understand the psychotic, but to grasp the dynamics of a social process as it is manifested in a family, and they suggest several interesting concepts pertaining to the dynamics of the family which we will italicize as we use them. The most important of these is that of *alliances*, which are formed when two people cooperate in doing something to another.

Their argument in *Sanity, Madness and the Family* is that in the families of the schizophrenics which were studied (there are eleven such families discussed in the book), the parents often form alliances with each other (p. 122) in order to support each other. From Laing's other books we can see that the kind of support that is vital involves *confirming* the other's sense of identity.[3] The parents are confused, ambivalent, and insecure enough (pp. 158-60) so that they often do one thing and say another to the child (p. 40), and then support each other in this kind of activity, sometimes even to the point of outright deception. Together they exert pressure on the child to get the child to accept *attributions* (p. 122), which consist of the parents' view of things (of the child, of the world). These parental attributions may be *disjunctive* with the child's own perceptions and feelings (p. 29), but the combination of the child's weak position and the parents' stronger position and the added power they get from their alliance with one another combine to create a situation where the child submits to the power of the parental attribution. This usually means that the child's own *identity* is endangered; his own existence is *invalidated* (p. 93). Invalidation can mean that one person is not supporting another, or that a person is actually telling another that she or he is wrong in feeling, thought, memory, perception. This childhood pattern is ex-

3. For example, see Chapter 8 in *Self and Others* (the original edition).

emplified by this statement by one of the diagnosed schizophrenics: "I can't trust what I see. It doesn't get backed up. It doesn't get confirmed in any way—just left to drift, you know. I think that's probably what my trouble is. Anything I might say, it has no backing" (p. 58). Here the young woman is expressing exactly what Laing perceives as the heart of the problem: the child loses a sense of self, a sense of trust in her own sensory and cognitive capacities; her parents contradict her so often and so confuse her that she ends up schizophrenic.

We have emphasized the most crucial of the terms Laing uses in his social-psychological analysis of the family: alliances, confirming and invalidating the other's identity, attributions, and disjunction. In this book, his analysis has a rather simple, even elegant, structure. There are powerful parents (and the concept of power is necessary to his analysis, although he does not use the term), who together (in an alliance) inflict damage on the identity of their child. The damage occurs because the parents invalidate the child's identity, by failing to help the child, by undercutting the child's own perceptions, and by attributing to the child certain characteristics which suit the parents' needs but not the child's. The concept of power is necessary because the only way to understand the child's acceptance of these attributions is through his inferior psychological power.

Implicit in this theory, although not stated explicitly, is a view of personal identity arising from or influenced importantly by relations with others. A person's sense of himself derives greatly from his relations with others: if others' perceptions do not tally with his own, if there is conflict, then identity formation is affected. Conflict, then, is a root notion, a core idea for Laing: in this book, the portraits are of families in conflict, with the parents inevitably aligned against the child. This picture will become more complicated in Laing's later books.

Another notion implicit in Laing's analysis is that people are born weak, needing help. If they do not get the help they need—if they do not get the support, the confirmation by others, which is vital to the achievement of a strong sense of identity—then people suffer. In his book, the focus is on the suffering, of course, on the experiences of the schizophrenics. But although Laing is concerned exclusively with—as it were—bad parenting in this book, we can infer his belief that good parenting is required if a newborn human is to grow and prosper. The explicit argument states only that bad parenting can hurt a child, but we can infer that Laing believes that some kind of "right" environment is necessary for a child's healthy growth.

Yet another implicit notion is that each of us is born with certain needs, attributes, gifts, talents, and potentials. Somehow out of these slowly arises our own *Weltanschauung,* which at first is particularly fragile and vulnerable to attack from others. Laing seems to believe that this gradual perception of the world needs to be nurtured if it is to grow strong; underneath his strong concern with the possibility of disconfirmation and invalidation is his belief that others can either fail to help us develop our own perceptions out of our own needs, or—even worse—can foist their perceptions of us on us. Thus, underlying Laing's analysis is a concept that I earlier called an *own need* (Marcuse). If one's own needs are not respected, then in this view, identity fails to develop, and schizophrenia is born.

4. *Self and other.* In a later book, *The Politics of the Family,* Laing offers a more complicated view of this topic; that problems arise in living not just because a few confused, disturbed people perpetuate their own confusion by mixing up their children (who are later called schizophrenic), but rather because we all *operate* on each other all the time in confusing ways. In this more complicated view, we are all both tormentor and victim, although Laing would doubtless still maintain that some people are victims more than others.

The tone of this latter book is more complicated. At times Laing seems to be simply compassionate: he describes people who hurt one another and who do so often without any clear recognition of what is going on; he shows us people caught up in reciprocal suffering, unable to extract themselves from the circle of pain. But at other times he seems angry, presumably at people who continue to hurt one another, as if they could stop the hurting if they chose. This anger is clearest in the earlier book, *The Politics of Experience*, where there are frequent references to the bombing in Vietnam, to the industrial-military complex (p. 49), to his view that "we are all murderers and prostitutes" (p. 11). His anger may be his chief attraction for some readers—characteristically those who have only read *The Politics of Experience*—but it is far from his usual tone, and in some of his books it is not visible at all.

In The Politics of the Family, he makes several points which need brief discussion. First, Laing's ideas about *fantasy*. In this book, to some extent in *Interpersonal Perception* (co-authored with R. Phillipson and A. R. Lee), and in *Self and Others*, Laing states that there are different modes of experience, and that the fantasy mode often interpenetrates with the apperceptive mode. He wants to argue that a sense of reality is a characteristic which can accompany any mode of experience. In *Self and Others*, he argues for four modes of experience (pp. 11 ff.),[4] but what is crucial is not the precise number, but rather that Laing is trying to get away from a simpleminded distinction between fantasy and reality. Here he is engaged with what ordinarily would be called phenomenological or metapsychological issues, trying to conceptualize distinctions in experience. One of the major points is that there are fantasy elements in most of our experience most of the time.

In part this is orthodox psychoanalytic thinking, but Laing goes beyond it in arguing that what are usually called psychological defense mechanisms can be seen as not just *intra*personal (as is conventional), but as transactional or *inter*personal. Thus my fantasies get tied up not just with my own thinking, and not just with my perception of you, but with *our* relationship and thus, inevitably, with you. Returning to parental alliances in the families of schizo-

4. But in the revised edition of this book, he seems to say that there are only three modes (memory, imagination, and perception), and that fantasy and reality are *qualities* which can distinguish any of these modes (*Self and Others*, revised edition, p. 11).

phrenics, Laing argues that a parent can project fantasy onto a child, and then force that child to embody that projection (Laing is interested in the *projected-upon*). But now Laing says that this happens not only in families of schizophrenics, but in all families; and in his other books (particularly *Interpersonal Perception* and *Self and Others*), he argues that this goes on in any dyadic (two-person) relationship:

> Pure projection is not enough. As images of ghostly relations under the operation of projection, we induce others, and are ourselves induced, to *embody* them: to enact, unbeknown to ourselves, a shadow play, as images of images of images . . . of the dead, who have in their turn embodied and enacted such dramas projected upon them, and induced in them, by those before them (PF, p. 78).

He clearly extends the analysis presented in *Sanity, Madness and the Family:* now his picture is not just of a parental alliance wreaking various kinds of harm on relatively helpless children, but of *all* parents doing unto their children as they in turn were done unto by their own parents, and so on, ad infinitum. Not only is the child "born into a family which is the project of the operations of human beings already in this world" (PF, p. 11), but this situation is multi-generational (cf. PF, pp. 53-57).[5]

Another vivid example from Laing will make this clear. He is discussing a man named Paul: "His body was a sort of mausoleum, a haunted graveyard in which the ghosts of several generations still walked, while their physical remains

5. Of course, other social scientists have made similar observations. Jules Henry's book *Pathways to Madness*, although devoted to the study of particular families and interactions within them, makes clear to some extent that the patterns of interaction within a family are related to earlier patterns characteristic of the grandparents. And Erik Erikson, in *Childhood and Society*, for example, tries to indicate how treatment of children is linked through the parents to their own treatment as children, and linked further to other surrounding events in a very complex and intricate way.

rotted away. This family had buried their dead *in each other*" (PF, p. 57). The references to people rotting away and burying their dead in one another lends a macabre dimension to Laing's conception at this point, and the idea becomes perhaps too clear. Laing views life as a drama in which people play roles. The people may change, but the roles remain constant:

> We can just glimpse in this family (an example Laing has given) a drama perpetuated over three generations—the players are two women and a man: first, mother, daughter, and father: second, mother, daughter, and daughter's son. Daughter's father dies—daughter conceives a son, *to replace* her father. The play's the thing. The actors come and go. As they die, others are born. The system perpetuates itself over generations: the young are introduced to the parts that the dead once played (PF, p. 29).

All of this can occur, Laing argues, because of the capacity for internalization and fantasy. Internalization refers to the way what is outside is assimilated: " 'Internalization' means to map 'outer' onto 'inner' " (PF, p. 7). This again is a conventional psychoanalytic notion, and Laing simply places it more firmly within the social context.

Laing believes family relations are permeated by a large element of fantasy: people overlay their perceptions of others with images of how they want those others to be, and how they think they ought to be. Often, of course, one's perception of how another ought to be is based on and rooted in his perception of some *significant other* earlier in one's life. Thus, a man may want his wife to act toward him as his mother acted toward his father. All of this can be, and often is unconscious. Laing devotes himself precisely to such questions of misperception between husbands and wives in his book *Interpersonal Perception*, which is laden with concrete examples of how complicated a "simple" dyadic relation can be. Each partner has perceptions of himself or herself, perceptions of the other, perceptions of how the other ought to be, perceptions of how the other perceives him, ideas about how the other ought to perceive him, and so on, indefinitely. The point for Laing is always how these different kinds of perceptions become interwoven in what is primarily an undifferentiated tangle resulting in sporadic outbursts of deep emotion when one of the partners violates some expectation of the other which resides so far within that neither person is conscious of its existence. Of course, as our perceptions get embodied in our behavior toward the other, they affect him: both his behavior and his experience of himself.

Thus people internalize both images of others and images of relations to others; and these images are not always in tune with reality, so that fantasy can be said to interpenetrate and infuse all interpersonal relations. Furthermore, Laing argues that all of this influences not just one's relations to others but one's relation to himself. Here we have one of the themes of *Sanity, Madness and the Family* (as well as of *The Divided Self*) where Laing shows young women losing themselves (becoming schizophrenic) because of the various kinds of family situations in which they lived. As Laing says, "Persons do manifestly try to act on the 'inner' worlds of others to preserve their own inner worlds; and others . . . arrange and rearrange the external world of objects to preserve their inner worlds" (PF, p. 13). This is the element Laing adds to Freud's picture of people: Laing shows people trying to affect the inner worlds of others in order to preserve their own inner worlds.

An example of the way in which Laing often portrays all this as inevitable: "As soon as we convey in any way (by a gesture, a handshake, a cough, a smile, an inflection of our voice) what we see or think we see, some change is occurring even in the most rigid situation" (PF, p. 40). Here he argues that all relationship with others involves articulating (verbally or otherwise) a sense of what is going on, and that the very articulation alters what is going on in one way or another. We have seen that his word for one aspect of this is *induction:*

Such inductions are going on, in my view, all the time. All our actions and reactions to the other imply some co-efficient of induction. We very seldom ever entirely relate absolutely accurately to the other. And indeed very seldom is there another there to whom one could. We make a gesture, that is itself an induced embodiment of an image of another projected upon oneself by another . . . (PF, p. 120).

Laing states clearly that not only are we doing something to someone else, but that what we do is a function of what was done to us earlier. Not only are we confusing the other, but we are doing so out of our own confusions.

The ideas here are not much different from those in *Sanity, Madness and the Family*, but he is broadening his scope, so that now he is talking about all of us, not just schizophrenic young women. When he expresses anger about this situation now, he must direct it not only against the parents of the schizophrenics (for being confused and destructive), but against all of us. Thus "The whole of our present civilization may be a captivity" he says (PF, p. 57); and he is led to make the usual comparisons of social life to hypnosis: "Under hypnosis, he feels it; and does not know that he has been hypnotized to feel it. How much of what we ordinarily feel, is what we have all been hypnotized to feel?" (PF, p. 79). Upset, Laing refers to the "almost complete holocaust of one's experience on the altar of conformity" and to the "normal social lobotomy" (PF, p. 101). And further, in comparing what we do to each other with what we do to the animals we eat, he says:

We like the food served up elegantly before us; we do not want to know about the animal factories, the slaughterhouses, and what goes on in the kitchen. Our own cities are our own animal factories; families, schools, churches are the slaughterhouses of our children; colleges and other places are the kitchens. As adults in marriages and business, we eat the product (PF, pp. 101-2).

From this perspective Laing might simply stop writing entirely and resign from the human race. As he says elsewhere: "Few books today are forgivable. Black on the canvas, silence on the screen, an empty white sheet of paper, are perhaps feasible. There is little conjunction of truth and social 'reality' . . . in the society of man, the truth resides now less in what things are than in what they are not" (PE, p. 11).[6] We are all insane: "We are bemused and crazed creatures, strangers to our true selves, to one another, and to the spiritual and material world—and, even, from an ideal standpoint we can glimpse but not adopt" (PE, p. 12).

5. *Laing's ideal: personal autonomy.* Laing portrays people as deeply confused about themselves, as grasping for reassurance about who they are and, in doing so, trying to get others to submit to various attributions which will help shore up their own sense of self. Thus, out of our own insecurity, we do things to others which confuse them. And the things we do to others—the projections we force them to embody, the images we want them to bring to life—are as often as not based on our own unconscious fantasies about ourselves and others, a process of which Laing is deeply critical.

When he refers to an ideal which we can glimpse but not adopt, what might he have in mind? A word which he uses frequently, and honorifically, perhaps locates the ideal realm he has in mind: autonomy.

In order to clarify the importance of personal autonomy to Laing's work, let us briefly review some of his discussion in another book, *The Divided Self*, in which he describes the experience of schizophrenics. Near the beginning he states that "a patient's disorganization is a failure to achieve a specifically personal form of unity . . . " (p. 24), and a lot of his analysis of schizophrenics revolves around his conception of the false self. Laing sets up a dichotomy between a true and a false self and argues that there is both a "normal" form of false self and a schizoid form, which is much more malignant. In his view, the false self of the normal is (a) not

6. PE: *The Politics of Experience.*

felt so intensely to be alien (as is the schizoid false self); (b) is not so compulsive and autonomous in the sense that the person does not feel out of control; and (c) does not preclude the emergence of spontaneous expression (pp. 95 ff.). Laing states that his conception of a false self does not neatly differentiate schizophrenics from everyone else, so that, as with Freud's concept of repression, the distinction resides in the matter of degree. Laing admits that normal people have false selves which seem to resemble those of schizophrenics:

> Besides the more or less permanent "personality" displayed by the false-self system, it may be, as we mentioned, the prey to innumerable transitory identifications on a small scale. . . . The transitory acquisition of small fragments of other people's behavior is not exclusively a schizoid problem, but it does tend to occur with particular insistence and compulsiveness on the basis of the schizoid false-self system (pp. 105-6).

So the schizophrenic's false self functions dynamically like the normal's false self, but is a bigger problem in various ways.

When Laing talks of "transitory acquisition of small pieces of others' behavior," we see a connection between what Laing is saying here and what he has said before. Here Laing shows how schizophrenics lose their sense of self, and he has a simpler conception of that problem than he develops later. In this book, he argues that schizophrenics lose their sense of self as a result of routine psychological processes (internalization, projection, and other operations which we perform on one another). But his view seems quite simply that schizophrenia occurs because of what has been done *to* them. They have been lied to, or conspired against; and at times he even argues that because we see them as different, they become different, and we see them as different in order to preserve our own fragile sense of self. This latter argument is part of his questioning the whole concept of schizophrenia. As part of this argument, Laing suggests that a person becomes psychotic when he loses a conflict with someone else in which he and the other have disjunctive perceptions.

From this argument we can infer that Laing prefers relationships in which people do not conflict violently, but support one another and derive a mutual sense of confirmation. He refers to the *true self* and to *autonomy* in ways which make it clear that he thinks each of us has a self to be true to, but from which we are often detoured by others. Although he leaves this matter of the *ideal* fundamentally unclear, we can see that the brief glimpses he gives of this ideal realm are remarkably similar to that part of Marcuse's ideal which stresses personal autonomy. Both men believe that autonomy is desirable, and both men seem to connect the idea of autonomy with the idea of hewing closer to one's own needs than to the desires of others. Autonomy clearly has something to do with not being bound too closely by others.

WHAT RELATION EXISTS BETWEEN LAING'S THOUGHT AND GENERAL SOCIAL CRITICISM?

Laing's name has become identified with an attack on certain social institutions, on conventional therapy, the mental-illness establishment, and, more importantly, on the family.

The harm done people by prisons is well known. When we read such analyses of prisons, we are bothered; but since our expectations about prisons are not very high to begin with, we may not be extremely shocked. But when social institutions like the school, the family, and the mental hospital are discussed in the same way, when writers argue that these institutions also do more harm than good for people, then we sit up and take some notice. We expect the family, the school, and the mental hospital to help people in one way or another.

This is particularly true with regard to families. Even though everyone may have some bad feelings which center on family experiences, and though most of us have become accustomed to thinking about psychotherapy as leading inevitably to malignant corners of family life, we still generally do not expect to be told that families do far more harm than good to people. Thus when Laing (and others) write about families, arguing that they cause immense suffering and do very little good by way of compensation for the suffering, we pay attention.

Laing is certainly a social critic in a general sense, at least some of the time. He says harsh things about the family and about many of our social institutions. Like Marcuse, he holds up our present way of life for comparison with a more ideal way, and our present way is found wanting. Further, both Laing and Marcuse seem to believe optimistically that the ideal life is attainable.

Social criticism in Laing and Marcuse would seem to have been carried as far as it can go. Once we have reached the point of recognizing the complete oppression and insanity of everyone (as some of the passages quoted from each man illustrate,) then what more is to be said? What is most interesting, perhaps, is that this kind of social criticism is rather popular. Such extreme views would seem appropriate only to people on the verge of suicide or random violence (as in Dostoevsky's novel, *The Possessed*, for example; or as in a few people around us). But how can such views become popular with large numbers of people? Part of the answer lies in the attractiveness of the ideal which Marcuse and Laing hold up, the ideal of personal autonomy. This ideal has a very strong appeal to us; there is a strong tendency in American culture away from social constraint and toward the development of an autonomous independent self. (I shall explore this more fully in the concluding chapter of this book.) The form of social criticism we are exploring here has at its roots, we will argue, a concern not with mundane goals such as spreading the wealth more equitably, but rather the creation of a world in which truly autonomous selves could survive and even prosper.

CRITICAL EVALUATION OF LAING'S THOUGHT

1. The family and psychosis.

Laing's writings on the family have two aims: first, to portray the family as in some cases being the creator of one kind of psychosis, namely schizophrenia; second, to describe family dynamics and processes in a more general sense, as they might occur in every family whether or not psychosis arises from the process. Separating these two goals is somewhat artificial: sometimes Laing says that we are all crazy, in which case the families of psychotics are no longer a special group, but instead, typical of all families. This is the first point at which we must draw attention to a crucial ambiguity in Laing, for he never really makes himself clear on this issue; he says different things in different books, and one has difficulty knowing which to believe.

The same ambiguity resides in Laing's discussion of psychosis as in his analysis and description of schizophrenic experience in *The Divided Self*. Here, too, he seems to waver between two different points of view. He says that a person is called psychotic when he disagrees with too many sane people, and he also says that a person who disagrees with others becomes psychotic as a result of what the others do to him after the disagreement occurs. Perhaps the problem in this book is that Laing moves back and forth between discussing what a schizophrenic experiences and analyzing how he got that way. Laing's description of the schizophrenic experience is rather powerful, but ultimately he never answers the crucial question of how different schizophrenic experience is from other forms of experience. This problem is rooted in his failure to clarify how schizophrenics become schizophrenic. Do ordinary babies become schizophrenics as a result of living in particularly unfavorable family environments while they are young, or are ordinary adults rather arbitrarily sorted into the schizophrenic category because of some surface disagreement with a powerful person? And that then, as a result of being treated as schizophrenics, they become schizophrenic—different from the rest of us? Or is it that even though we call them schizophrenic, they remain essentially no different from the rest of us, save that they have this label stuck to them? Laing seems to make all these arguments at different points.

The confusion is compounded when a number of his books are read together; then we see that Laing argues that schizophrenics are not different from the rest of us, save that they have been subjected to an arbitrary labeling process whose dynamics can be explained entirely in terms of the person doing the labeling. He further argues that schizophrenics are better than the rest of us (wiser, holy, filled with light and truth); then he argues they are worse off than the rest of us, because they are unusually confused due to a very insidious form of torment they have undergone in childhood.

Our focus here is on conceptual confusions, rather than methodological ones: the methodological drawbacks of Laing's studies of the families of schizophrenics are not crucial to our attempt to read him as a conceptual theorist (these drawbacks have been well discussed elsewhere; see, for example, Mishler's excellent discussion). However, I should at least point out that until Laing studies normal families as he has the families of psychotics, he will not be able to talk legitimately about what makes psychotic families different from normal ones; and even then, of course, he will not have any way of knowing whether the observed differences (if there are any) are what caused the psychosis earlier.

On the conceptual level, however, let us draw attention to the weakness of his attempt to provide a vocabulary and conceptual structure for analyzing the nexus of a family. Although Laing says that a more social-psychological kind of understanding is needed, he never fulfills the promise provided by the concept of nexus. He never really goes beyond simply showing how one person can hurt another, especially when the person doing the hurting is older and psychologically more powerful than the other, as in a family where the parent is more powerful than the child, and as, to some extent, in almost any human interaction.

However, the concept of a parental alliance is a truly social-psychological concept, although the descriptions of alliances fall far short of the original ambition to describe the nexus of family dynamics. What we have instead is essentially a situation in which one person or two people together cooperate in driving another person (usually a child) crazy. This is the portrait Laing and Esterson provide. In many places they state that instead of describing truly social dynamics in the group sense, they are simply showing how power is a dimension which permeates small group interactions, particularly dyadic ones (or *triadic*: three-person interactions). They merely shift the focus from looking at the disturbed person (the psychotic) to looking at what they see as the disturbing person; as they comment in a footnote (SMF, p. 149) conventional psychiatry has "clinical terms for disturbed, but not for disturbing persons"; and they seem interested in rectifying this imbalance. But obviously, pointing one's finger at a disturbing person rather than a disturbed person does not really elucidate family or social dynamics. However, Laing has surely broadened his scope to include a study of how people influence each other, not just in driving one another crazy, but more generally.

2. Self and other.

Laing's main contribution to our understanding social interaction is pointed at by his important use of the concepts of fantasy, internalization, projection, confirmation, and invalidation. He sees each of us as having (or being through) many modes of experience. Sometimes a mode of experience has certain fantasy elements. Laing's conceptual weakness lies in never making powerful distinctions between various modes of experiencing (see the earlier discussion, page 97 above), nor does he make very clear exactly what he means by fantasy. Generally, we can see that his use of the term *fantasy* derives from psychoanalytic thinking, and thus probably refers to thought that has a more intensive relation to inner needs, feelings, drives, than to outer objects and people. Laing erodes the distinction between reality experiencing and fantasy experiencing, arguing that fantasy interpenetrates most of our experiencing.

Second, Laing argues that much of our image of ourselves, of the world, and of other people involves internalization and projection; we take into ourselves (psychologically) parts of other people, and we project parts of ourselves, of the world, and of other people involves intertain characteristics to others as we project parts of our own perceptions and fantasies onto them, which often strongly affects other people.

Finally, Laing's concepts of confirmation and invalidation make clear that each person's sense of self is powerfully affected by other people; other people either help us solidify our own sense of self (confirm us), or they do the opposite (invalidate us). Invalidation can refer to positive acts of harm, as when one person calls the other "stupid" and thus helps to make him stupid; or it can involve simply failing to help the other, as when he says something to you and you ignore him.

Laing's discussion and elaboration of these concepts demonstrate that such interpersonal processes go on constantly, and there is no avoiding them. However, part of his thought arises from a fierce concern for personal autonomy which seems to run counter to the picture of interpersonal interaction he presents simultaneously. For there is a real sense in which his use of concepts like internalization, projection, confirmation, and invalidation questions the whole concept of personal autonomy.

3. Personal autonomy.

Underlying Laing's discussion of families and the effect of earlier generations on later generations as the later generations internalize not just images of their parents but images of how their parents relate to one another, is a fierce concern for personal autonomy. This concern for autonomy underlies all his work, from *The Divided Self* to his latest talks. But given the importance of what he calls internalization, of projection and confimation, then to what extent can we speak of any person as autonomous, as unique, original, distinct from his forebears?

In *The Divided Self*, Laing seems to posit an ideal relationship in which two people confirm one another's sense of
identity: "when two sane persons meet, there appears to be
a reciprocal recognition of each other's identity" (p. 35).
But in such a relationship, although the event that Laing
finds so destructive is avoided (disconfirmation), there is
serious question whether any autonomy is achieved. For as
Laing states in the books we have already discussed, one's
own sense of self is often a product of *operations* that have
been performed on one by others earlier. Given that, and
given his view of people continually doing things to each
other in everyday life to modify both the other's and one's
own sense of self, then how is it possible to talk in any
simple way of one's sense of identity?

Here Laing is in conceptual difficulty. In *The Divided
Self*, he starts to show how the schizophrenic has a false self
which is contrasted with a true self. He talks at length about
that false self, about ontological insecurity and the various
forms of anxiety which he thinks characterize the schizoid
false self. He describes in detail relationships in which a
false self is foisted on a person by another, a topic that he
discusses again in *Sanity, Madness and the Family*. He
occasionally refers to relationships in which this does not
occur, as in the passage quoted above about "reciprocal
recognition of each other's identity," but he never is very
specific about this, and his talk of autonomy and identity is
largely disconnected from his concrete examples. All his
examples are of false selves; and sometimes he even implies
that ontological insecurity (one of the hallmarks of the false
self) is becoming a characteristic of modern society (he
refers rather sweepingly to Kafka, Beckett, and modern
literature in general [7]). But in general he seems to think
that the schizophrenic is different from the rest of us by
virtue of the extremity of the false-self system in him.

But Laing later repudiates this notion, explicitly in a
preface to a new edition of *The Divided Self*: ". . . today I
feel that, even in focusing upon and attempting to delin-

7. See Chapter 3 of *The Divided Self*, especially pp. 39-41.

eate a certain type of schizoid existence, I was already partially falling into the trap I was seeking to avoid. I am still writing in this book too much about Them, and too little about Us." [8] He repudiates it implicitly in much of his later writing, which is devoted to dissecting the various ways in which each of us embodies and is embodied in the other. Thus, not only schizophrenics lose their true self; we all do, and the process appears almost inevitable at times. But that, of course, is the question.

In *The Divided Self*, Laing seems, although faintly, to hold a notion of authentic human existence. He does not identify it, but it underlies much of what he says. And in *The Politics of Experience*, he clearly holds that human beings are born with capacities for growth which are then stifled. This book is more rhetoric than analysis, but many of the ideas that he details more closely in his other books are here: the interpenetrations of selves, induction, people creating images of themselves and influencing the images of others. But his focus has shifted: now schizophrenics are doing better than the rest of us; they are expressing their vivid sense of the rottenness of life. By suffering, they may be winning through to existence on a higher human plane. The indictment here is of our civilization:

> From the moment of birth, when the stone-age baby confronts the twentieth-century mother, the baby is subjected to these forms of violence, called love, as its mother and father have been, and their parents and their parents before them. These forces are mainly concerned with destroying most of its potentialities. This enterprise is on the whole successful. By the time the new human being is fifteen or so, we are left with a being like ourselves. A half-crazed creature, more or less adjusted to a mad world. This is normality in our present age (PE, p. 50).

But even in this sweeping indictment in which love is seen

8. Preface to the 1965 Pelican edition of *The Divided Self*, p. 11.

as violence, in which everything and everybody stands condemned, there seems to be some notion, however unformulated, that things need not be this way. Laing believes that people have potential and presumes that there must be a way to liberate it instead of destroying it. Elsewhere he expresses his faith that there is in each of us some authentic *I* buried amid the rubble:

> In the last resort, it is perhaps never true to say that the "self" has been utterly lost, or destroyed, even in the most "dilapidated hebephrenic" to use H. S. Sullivan's appropriately horrible term. There is still an "I" that cannot find a "me." An "I" has not ceased to exist, but it is without substance, it is disembodied, it lacks the quality of realness, and it has no identity, it has no "me" to go with it. (*The Divided Self*, p. 171).

But a recurrent message throughout his writings is that there is no truly isolated self or *I*:

> We see that in a dyadic system, there is no isolated individual person. The one person, in order to maintain his own self-identity, has to act towards the other.... At best this intimate intermeshed coexistence can be reciprocally confirmatory; at worst it is a mishmash in which both can lose themselves ... (*Interpersonal Perception*, p. 35).

As Laing says here, "at best" it is reciprocally confirmatory; given his own perception of the extent to which fantasy permeates our own sense of self and other, mutual confirmation is as likely to be *folie à deux* as ascent to higher Truth. As he puts this in the jargon of psychology, even total conjunction between two people only gains reliability, not validity (*Interpersonal Perception*, p. 29).

On the one hand, Laing argues that each of us operates on ourselves and others through images which are as likely as not to be imbued with fantasy. On the other hand, he argues that autonomy is desirable. But whence autonomy?

Given the persuasiveness of Laing's analysis of dyadic and familial interaction, surely radical autonomy is a chimera; one wonders why Laing desires it so fiercely.

Perhaps Laing's insistence on the need for radical autonomy is part and parcel of that disease of Western civilization which he is so fond of discussing. Laing's clear view of mutual dependency, coupled with his insistence on becoming autonomous, strikes one as Western individualism carried to fever pitch: "If an individual needs another in order to be himself, it presupposes a failure fully to achieve autonomy, i.e., he engages in life from a basically insecure ontological position (*The Divided Self*, p. 186). For Philip Slater, who analyzes the American pursuit of loneliness,[9] this might seem an archetypal statement of the American neurosis. Laing seems to say that needing others is a sign of weakness and failure, a strange view for a psychiatrist to take.

But in a sense, Laing's conclusion is a logical outcome of his thought. He begins studying schizophrenics and, out of distrust of conventional psychiatry, looks for social sources of their maladies. After locating some of the schizophrenic's problems in a particular social context (the family), Laing studies "normal" psychological processes and finds, too, the same kind of dynamics he had discovered in the families of schizophrenics. At this point, Laing has two choices: he can and does decide to integrate his psychological views with a thoroughgoing criticism of our society; Lionel Trilling argues in *Sincerity and Authenticity* this may have been inevitable. Once a causative connection between schizophrenia and social factors had been "established with any semblance of plausibility" it was inevitable that

the characterization of society that followed from it should be of an ultimately pejorative kind: society was to be thought of, not as civilization's agent exacting for the good of human development a price that was high yet not finally beyond what the means of the race

9. Philip Slater, *The Pursuit of Loneliness* (Boston: Beacon Press, 1970).

might afford, but as the destroyer of the very humanity it pretended to foster (Trilling, p. 168).

Laing has gone beyond this line of thought to the point of glorifying psychosis as a means of fighting the malignancy of civilization or as a way of escaping from an intolerable world. Trilling comments justly about this aspect of Laing's thought:

> But who that has spoken, or tried to speak, with a psychotic friend will consent to betray the masked pain of his bewilderment and solitude by making it the paradigm of liberation from the imprisoning false-hoods of an alienated social reality? (p. 171)

Trilling errs, perhaps, in seeing this aspect of Laing's thought as central; it may be tangential, for it does not flow necessarily from most of his published writings, even though his popularity may rest on his views of the holiness of madness.

There is another direction Laing might have taken (and still might take) from his earlier published work. Leaving aside *The Politics of Experience* and examining his other published volumes, we might see him as ready to proceed as Freud did. Having located certain psychological dynamics which characterize both dyadic relations and familial relations and having linked these both to schizophrenic and normal experience, Laing might differentiate the way these dynamics occur in different families and different people. Instead of arguing that schizophrenics are just like the rest of us except that they are treated worse by others, he might proceed with what he began so well in *The Divided Self* and *Sanity, Madness and the Family*. He might formulate how these dynamics—which might, like Freud's repression, be conceived of as universal—occur differentially in different situations. This, too, would be consistent with much, if not all, of his published work.

Of course, Laing would still have a conceptual problem with autonomy if he chose to retain that as an "ideal" life;

he will not find it easy to characterize an autonomy which is consistent with his other psychological views. Despite his railing about the corrosion of the self, he has done as much as anyone to show the inevitability of some degree of corrosion.

CONCLUSIONS

The problems inherent in the concept of radical or extreme personal autonomy are obvious. If we are to retain a concept of autonomy, as both Laing and Marcuse seem to think important, then we must modify our understanding of autonomy, to leave room for a substantial amount of interpersonal influence. We will need to move beyond a simpleminded distinction between conformity, on the one hand, and autonomy on the other. This theme will be explored at greater length in the next chapter in the work of Erving Goffman. As we continue, let us keep in mind Laing's important descriptions of people as needing one another confirmation, as intertwined in one another through images and internalizations and projections, many of which derive from rather complicated networks of relations which we each have with other people from the very moment of birth. Especially let us consider Laing's underlining of the importance of our weakness at birth, another of his central (if implicit) contributions. He shows us the baby born into a world of powerful adults, being inevitably affected by them in ways beyond its control.

CHAPTER 5

Erving Goffman:
The Constraints of Sociability

Moving from Laing to Goffman involves moving further into a consideration of the difficulty of freeing the self from the world of constraining sociality. For although Laing seems to hold out the hope that such a freeing is possible (although his own thinking actually undercuts that hope), Goffman quite clearly insists that each of us is unavoidably caught up in a social network; and he hints that the very existence of a self in each of us, a self capable of feeling opposed to the surrounding social world, is possible only when there is sustained contact with that surrounding social world.

Yet Goffman shares with both Marcuse and Laing some remnant of an attitude of bewilderment that this should be so. He occasionally wishes—admittedly tenuously—that the self should not be so constrained, that in a better world the self would be triumphant over the outside forces which press in upon it. This contrast between his lucid description of the societal toils within which any person is entangled and his wish that this not be the case, will be underlined in the following analysis of his thinking.

Erving Goffman is a sociologist whose published work has been accumulating over the past twenty years. I shall not attempt to review each of his eight books, but just lay bare some of the underpinnings. His work is of a piece. His eight books all deal with the same topics and thus lend them-

116

selves readily to an interpretive analysis of several major themes. His field is social interaction, particularly interaction between two people. He explores the ways in which people define situations together and the ways in which the structure of their own selves arises out of and is rooted in these situational definitions.

The point of our discussing Goffman is to indicate that there do exist social-psychological ideas which can help us gain a clearer view of the relations between self and society and which can also pinpoint the crucial points at which any coherent and general social-psychological theory must say something. Thus we are not only introducing some readers to the work of a fascinating sociologist, not only attempting to show certain ways in which his theoretical formulations fail to fit together so neatly as they ought to; but we are also helping ourselves construct a viable social-psychological theory. As usual, we shall discuss most intensively those topics which are pertinent to earlier discussion: the ideas of autonomy and authenticity will again come up in this chapter, as well as later in the book.

GOFFMAN'S WORK

1. Method: examples and conceptual analysis.

Goffman's approach to social interaction is exclusively observational and conceptual: he accumulates observations from daily life, literature, books, and articles; then attempts to abstract some general principles, from the observations; or he presents some general principles and then attempts to illustrate them by observations he has accumulated.

Goffman tries to provide a more coherent conceptual model of the relation between self and society, one which will have descriptive and explanatory power. He legitimizes this ambition at the beginning of his first published book by referring to Simmel, the well-known sociologist:

> The justification for this approach (as I take to be the justification for Simmel's also) is that the illustrations together fit into a coherent framework that ties to-

gether bits of experience the reader has already had and provides the student with a guide worth testing in case studies of institutional social life (PS, p. xii).[1]

This approach might be called philosophical by some modern proponents of the experimental method in psychology, and it would be meant pejoratively. Clearly science has its roots in careful observation and conceptual analysis as well as in experimentation; Goffman reverts to a temporarily outmoded tradition in offering careful observation and a coordinated intensive effort at systematic conceptual analysis which, among social psychologists, is perhaps most reminiscent of Fritz Heider or Kurt Lewin. Whatever tradition Simmel, Heider, and Lewin can be said to belong to, it is not one that is firmly rooted in American soil; all three of them were European by birth and education although Lewin and Heider came to America.[2]

Goffman's method is that of "unsystematic, naturalistic observation" as he says in his recent book (RP, p. xv)[3], and although he admits that this method has its very serious limitations, he claims in his own defense "that the traditional research designs thus far employed in this area have considerable limitations of their own" (RP pp. xv-xvi). His criticisms of conventional research are that generalizations are difficult to justify; that "the variables which emerge tend to be creatures of research design that have no existence outside the room in which the apparatus and subjects are located"; and perhaps, most telling, that such conventional research is characterized by conceptual poverty. In his words:

> Fields of naturalistic study have not been uncovered through these methods. Concepts have not emerged

1. PS: *The Presentation of Self in Everyday Life.*

2. There are American social psychologists interested in pursuing this line, but the only one I know who takes the "conceptual analysis" idea seriously is Joseph de Rivera (now at Clark University), who thus far has not published anything along these lines.

3. RP: *Relations in Public.*

that reorder our view of social activity. Frameworks have not been established into which a continuously larger number of facts can be placed. Understanding of ordinary behavior has not accumulated, distance has (RP, p. xvi).

Goffman strives for a reordering of our view of social activity; he searches for a framework within which facts can be organized. (This is an important feature of his work for me, since one of my aims in this book is to provide such a framework.)

2. Goffman's tone.

Goffman's style needs to be discussed if only because it is somewhat strange, not like that of the ordinary social scientist. Marshall Berman, in a review of Goffman's book *Relations in Public*, tries to compare Goffman to Kafka. That comparison alone, whether valid or not, suggests that Goffman's writing has some peculiarities.

In many respects Goffman is a man of our times. Part of his modern tone is his refusal to define reality; he ignores this problem in favor of describing how we each agree on certain definitions of reality and how these definitions change as social interactions change. His focus is on *how* we define reality, particularly social reality; as he says at the beginning of his first book, *The Presentation of Self in Everyday Life*, much of social life seems to be dedicated to avoiding open conflict over the issue of how to define reality; or to agreeing that one person's claim about that reality will be honored at one moment, another person's at another moment. He shows us a person acting as though reality is such and such; then he analyzes how one person's view of reality comes to be accepted or rejected by others, often through covert and implicit means. Thus he is concerned with a working consensus (PS, p. 10); he is interested in what happens when one person's definition of reality is discredited (whence his recurrent interest in phenomena of shame and embarrassment; or in people who are trying to protect one impression while covertly sustaining a different one).

A different but closely related point that fascinates Goffman is the fragility of such working consensus we manage to achieve in social life. This concern with the fragility of social relationships is a consequence of his neglect of reality in favor of the issue of how reality is defined. As soon as people are given responsibility for definitions of reality, as soon as the focus is on the perception of things rather than on the things themselves, then one is well on the way to being lost or concerned with being lost. Insofar as people are fragile, insofar as each person's view differs from that of others and conflict regarding definitions of reality is the order of the day, then one is concerned with fragility. And Goffman's concern with the fragility of our definitions of reality is central to all his work. In a peculiar way—in this sense he is perhaps hypermodern if the phrase makes any sense—he exaggerates the fragility of social relationships by choosing to focus on actors, on spies, on confidence men, on those who quite clearly and unequivocally pretend. It is precisely these people who are particularly worried about the dangers of being uncovered, of having their false mask destroyed. Goffman further argues that we are all like these people in that we all constantly construct various pretenses, various subterfuges, each of us constantly on the watch for people or circumstances which might disrupt our pretenses. Thus the world, as pictured in much of Goffman's writing (and this is particularly pronounced in the book that Berman reviewed) is a place full of potential danger. Each person must constantly be on the lookout, must constantly be wary lest he be uncovered, unmasked.

But what makes Goffman's tone bizarre is the combination of this emphasis on the fragility of social life and the tenuousness of our definitions of situation and self, with a general air of complete confidence. He does not seem worried about dangers; on the contrary, he sounds completely assured and confident. All his concern with the fragility of social relationships and the insubstantiality of our contact with reality is embodied in a text which exudes confidence and certainty. Goffman has a sure sense of self and of reality, he does not sound lost. This is an interesting enigma, and is the beginning of what might be a fruitful comparison of Goffman and certain modern novelists. Berman suggests Kafka, but other modern novelists and writers are better compared with Goffman; the contrast between tone and content is less to be found in Kafka than in Vonnegut, Barthelme, or Heller.

3. Ideas: Overview.

Marshall Berman accurately argued that Goffman is working out a vision of life (p. 1). We shall examine some of the essential constituents of that vision because Goffman has an approach to a view of the relation between man and society which might help us better comprehend the nature of social life.

Goffman's work can be seen as moving from two poles: his sense of the order and structure of the social interactions of everyday life; and his sense of the invisibility of the crucial terms of that order, namely the personal experience each of us has out of which the order grows and on which it rests. His published writing revolves around these two poles. On the one hand, he examines the structure of everyday social interaction, which leads him into analyzing minute examples of interaction. He takes his examples from novels, from sociological books and papers, and from everyday life. He tries to show us the structure underlying these events partly by giving us terms for analyzing these events, but he also tries to make clear the inferences hidden beneath the surface of the interaction.

Thus Goffman shows us that the surface has structure: the way people say hello to strangers in a given society can be described; and when he shows us the pattern, he follows what appears to be an anthropological or an ethological, tradition. But he also shows us—and here he is more psychological, philosophical, and literary—that some of the essential constituents of this external order are hidden processes going on within the participants in the social order. Because these processes are out of sight, submerged, hard to discern, they are not easily knowable; any knowledge we gain about them is likely to be mistaken; and much of what appears as the bizarre tone in Goffman's writing arises from his conviction that many of the important components of the social interactions in which we are all engaged daily are invisible. As he says at the beginning of his first book: "Many crucial facts lie beyond the time and place of interaction, or lie concealed within it (PS, p. 2)."

Ideas: Performance—the presentation of self. Much of Goffman's work shows that even the seemingly trivial daily interactions are ceremonial. "The world, in truth, is a wedding" (PS, p. 36). People are always on stage, as when they are with others; they are always putting on performances which aim toward an idealized image:

> Thus when the individual presents himself before others, his performance will tend to incorporate and exemplify the officially accredited values of the society, more so in fact, than does his behavior as a whole (PS, p. 35).

Here Goffman cites Cooley's having made the same point, and draws on Durkheim and Radcliffe-Brown, who were interested in ceremony "as an expressive rejuvenation and reaffirmation of the moral values of the community" (PS, p. 35). Clearly Goffman's focus in this book is not on the *self* which is being presented, but on the *presentation* as a function not of an internal self but as a function of external society, or of one's perceptions of that external society.

Goffman believes that each person's concentration on his performance leads to some misrepresentation of himself, some divergence between appearance (the way he looks to others) and reality. In his analysis (see PS, pp. 44-45, and elsewhere) Goffman argues that some discrepancy is inevitable insofar as a person remains in touch with the society of which he is a part, because any person is more complicated than the social norms and mores he is required to revere. *Complicated* here means, in part, made up of contradictory elements; and it also means inconsistent from moment to moment. As Goffman observes:

> As human beings, we are presumably creatures of variable impulse with moods and energies that change from one moment to the next. As characters put on for an audience, however, we must not be subject to ups and downs (PS, p. 56).

This makes the matter appear quite simple: each of us has changes of feeling, mood, attitude, from moment to moment; each of us differs from others to some extent; but social mores and rules do not change so swiftly, and they must be applicable to all in a given society. Thus each of us puts on performances which do some violence to inner truth in favor of upholding social norms. But the matter is more complicated, as Goffman makes clear in quoting from Santayana and Simone de Beauvoir on the pages just following the above excerpt. Each of us to some extent develops an image of how we want to be and then endeavors to make that image real by putting on a show or presentation to convince not only others but ourselves. Throughout Goffman's books there is clear evidence that he is concerned not only with how we present ourselves to others in such a way that others are fooled, but with how we fool ourselves as well. Nearly all his examples are of people who are fooling others and know it: spies who are very aware of the extent to which their presented self differs from their real self, actors, impersonators, and charlatans of various sorts. But a persistent theme running throughout his work is the difficulty of differentiating liars (like the British spy who is pretending to be a native German) from the rest of us:

> When we turn from outright impersonations and barefaced lies to other types of misrepresentation, the commonsense distinction between true and false impressions becomes even less tenable (p. 64). . . . In general, then, the representation of an activity will vary in some degree from the activity itself and there-

fore inevitably misrepresent it (p. 65). . . . While we
could retain the commonsense notion that fostered
appearances can be discredited by a discrepant reality,
there is often no reason for claiming that the facts
discrepant with the fostered impression are any more
the real reality than is the fostered reality they em-
barrass (PS, p. 65).

Notice that Goffman endeavors to retain a focus on the
problematic aspects of knowing others. How do we know
that a friend's offer of a loan is disinterested? In a sense, we
never do know truly, since our knowledge of others is indi-
rect; part of the time Goffman appears to be staying at this
level of analysis, stating the problems of decoding what
others do. One of Goffman's overall themes is that just as
we have difficulty in knowing whether the presentation of
someone else that we are seeing is a veridical reflection of his
true self, we simultaneously have difficulty in discerning our
own true selves.

However, Goffman also argues that this issue—what we
really are underneath the outward show—is not pertinent;
he wants to keep to his topic, to analyze appearances and
presentations. His central explicit argument is that each of
us must be concerned with performances, with how others
perceive us, regardless of whether we are overtly liars and
impersonators. Implicitly he argues that we have great
difficulty discerning where the truth lies in what we see of
others (and this leads rather impressively in *Relations in
Public* to what Berman calls the Kafkaesque tone); and
even more importantly, we have great difficulty in knowing
where the truth lies in what we see of ourselves, given that so
much of what we see of ourselves is a reflection (how we look
to others), and that each of us fluctuates so from moment to
moment.

Ideas: Teams. Goffman offers another way of ap-
proaching this issue when he discusses teams. In his
words: "I will use the term 'performance team' or, in short,
'team' to refer to any set of individuals who co-operate in

staging a single routine" (PS, p. 79). This becomes interesting when he says

> Given this point of reference, it is possible to assimi-
> late such situations as the two-person interaction into
> the framework by describing these situations as two-
> team interaction in which each team contains only one
> member (PS, p. 80).

Talking about one-member teams enables him to return to
the issue of self-deception; if a person has more than one
part, he can obviously both put on a performance and view
it; using the team analysis, Goffman can say that one
member of the team is performing and one member is
viewing, all the while making clear that both members in
this instance are part of a single person. At this point in his
analysis, Goffman provides a fascinating footnote which is
worth quoting in full:

> Individualistic modes of thought tend to treat pro-
> cesses such as self-deception and insincerity as charac-
> terological weaknesses generated within the deep
> recesses of the individual personality. It might be bet-
> ter to start from outside the individual and work in-
> ward than to start inside the individual and work out.
> We may say that the starting point for all that is to
> come later consists of the individual performer main-
> taining a definition of the situation before an audience.
> The individual automatically becomes insincere when
> he adheres to the obligations of maintaining a work-
> ing consensus and when he participates in different
> routines or performs a given part before different au-
> diences. Self-deception can be seen as something that
> results when two different roles, performer and au-
> dience, come to be compressed into the same indi-
> vidual (PS, footnote, p. 81).

One persistent theme in Goffman is his starting from the
outside, as he says, following the Chicago Cooley-Mead

sociological tradition. He views the self as inevitably fragmented into performer and viewer, into a team made up of
different entities. This view of the self is central to his
thought. Each of us is seen as playing a number of roles and
being fragmented thus. Moreover, each of us has fluctuating
feelings, and thus different points of view. Further, each of
us is capable of "taking the point of view of the other" (as
Mead insisted so long ago), and thus different stances with
regard to any given issue; and each different stance we can
take further fragments our internal organization. All of this
is seen as inevitable, as unavoidable, and quite definitely
not as immoral or dishonest or bad.

Ideas: Covertness of social interaction. Goffman is interested in why these performances are necessary. He offers
different kinds of answers to this question. We have already
discussed one answer: the performance ties the performer
into a social network by including within it some consideration of how others will view it. The performer is also
offering homage to one or another of a set of social mores
and norms; each time an individual reaffirms the norms, the
norms are solidified as an element uniting diverse people.

A different kind of answer is provided when Goffman
points out the covertness of much social interaction; as we
mentioned earlier, many of the crucial components of any
social event are not easily seen.

> The study of social events presents an almost insur-
> mountable difficulty, in that their visibility, as one
> might say, is very low. In social space, one's direct
> immediate capacity to see what is happening does not
> extend any further than one's own senses extend.
> Beyond that one has to make inferences based on
> hearsay evidence, reports of one kind or another of
> what other human beings are able to see within their
> equally limited field of observation (Laing, "The Ob-
> vious," p. 110).

This passage quoted is Laing's, but Goffman would agree
fully. Here the focus is on the limitations of one's observa-

tional field. One obvious limitation is that one cannot be in more than one place at once; another is that many crucial events are past, over with, and therefore hard to examine in detail. But Goffman's concern goes beyond this routine social scientist viewpoint; he is interested in the limitations imposed on us in situations where we are actually present, but where what the other person is doing is to some extent hidden, since all we can see is that protruding tip of the event, as it were. We cannot in any easy automatic way see the meaning of what the other person is doing, since seeing that meaning demands that we see what the other person is thinking and feeling. The covertness of thinking and feeling is Goffman's primary interest; that and the double difficulty posed by that covertness. One difficulty is that we may not really know what the other person is doing—is he really interested in me when he says "How are you?" and so on. But the related difficulty is that the other person may not know what we are up to, and we must take that fact into account in our behavior with him. This leads us often to what Goffman calls *a concern with dramatization*. We want to make especially sure, sometimes, that another person reads us clearly, understands us perfectly; and we go to special lengths to make sure our meaning is clear. This involves us in putting on a performance; when Goffman considers this, he naturally provides examples which are designed to make clear that no easy distinction is possible between such obviously performed situations and all others. Goffman argues that we are always to some extent concerned with making vivid what we mean, and no sooner are we engaged in contriving a set of signs for the other person to read so that he can get our meaning, than we are in acute danger of misusing this capacity or being misled by the other's misuse of this capacity. Once we enter into the show, then the possibility of deception always exists.

Ideas: The fractionated self. One central thrust of Goffman's thought is toward eroding our confidence in our natural idea of the individual as a coherent unified social participant. We have a psychology of individuals and we have a sociology of groups; but to get a social psychology of individuals-in-groups, we may need a concept which violates our conventional everyday understanding of what an individual is. What is an individual? A physical body with some psychological coherence, perhaps; ordinarily, we assume a considerable degree of continuity and sameness in an individual; but possibly we need a different conception of what an individual is if we are to make sense of much of social behavior. As Goffman says:

> In fine grain analysis, however, it may be that the notion of the individual as such will prove too imprecise, and instead a need will appear to use a variety of technically defined terms (RP, p. 27).

What alternative conception does Goffman offer? He never answers this question directly, but we can gather from his writings something of the way he might choose to handle the question. Instead of emphasizing the unity and coherence of the individual, he would emphasize the splitting and division of that individual. For example, he points out: that

> ... no matter what is done to the individual by way of punishment for crime, he is likely to have a moment free before the punishment is inflicted to proclaim identity with the powers whose ire is about to be visited upon him and to express separateness from the self upon whom the justice will fall (RP, p. 116).

Goffman goes on to say that this kind of occurrence can be seen as:

> ... but one expression of the "splitting" character of the self during interaction, that is, the general capacity of an individual to handle himself by stepping back from what he seems to have become in order to take up an alignment involving distance from this person;

and that, in turn, this capacity results from the inevitable interactional fact that that which comments on
what has happened cannot be what has happened. I
here attempt to derive a property of interactants from
interaction. My claim is that the individual is constituted so that he can split himself in two, the better to
allow one part to join the other members of an encounter in any attitude whatsoever to his other part
(RP, p. 117).

Here Goffman argues that the fact that an individual can
take different attitudes towards himself implies that an
individual is complicated, is divided into parts which can
act—to some degree—independently of one another. Notice
that Goffman's wording ("I here attempt to derive . . .")
implies that, in part, his attempt is conceptual; although his
books are full of examples, the point is always to analyze
and compare the examples so that sturdy applicable concepts will result.

Goffman's talk of selves splitting in parts most obviously
derives from Mead in sociology; in psychology, Freud's
name is most frequently invoked when selves are splitting;
for Laing's analysis of *The Divided Self* notwithstanding, it
is preeminently Freud who made the split self comprehensible, Freud who provided a framework within which talk of
divided selves seems sensible.

Ideas: Self and society. Goffman describes ways in which
the self arises from opposition to social pressures. In one of
the essays in *Asylums*, he says in several different ways that
"In every social establishment there are official expectations
as to what the participant owes the establishment" (*Asylums*,
p. 304), and that "Whenever we look at a social establishment, we find a counter to this first theme: we find that
participants decline in some way to accept the official view
of what they should be putting into and getting out of the
organization . . ." (p. 304). Much of his analysis of the bizarre behavior of patients in a mental hospital hinges on

this idea, that the patients are trying to stand apart from the institution in which they find themselves; they are trying to forge a sense of self and autonomy:

> The practice of reserving something of oneself from the clutch of an institution is very visible in mental hospitals and prisons but can be found in more benign and less totalistic institutions, too. I want to argue that this recalcitrance is not an incidental mechanism of defense but rather an essential constituent of the self. . . . We always find the individual employing methods to keep some distance, some elbow room, between himself and that with which others assume he should be identified . . . (*Asylums*, p. 319).

This point is interesting because it goes beyond the usual sociological view of the self as anchored in social relations, as wilting away without emotional support from groups (*Asylums*, p. 319). As Goffman says:

> The simplest sociological view of the individual and his self is that he is to himself what his place in an organization defines him to be. When pressed, a sociologist modifies this model by granting certain complications: the self may be not yet formed or may exhibit conflicting dedications. Perhaps we should further complicate the construct by elevating these qualifications to a central place, initially defining the individual, for sociological purposes, as a stance-taking entity, a something that takes up a position somewhere between identification with an organization and opposition to it, and is ready at the slightest pressure to regain its balance by shifting its involvement in either direction. It is thus *against something* that the self can emerge (*Asylums*, pp. 319-20).

But at the same time, Goffman is striving for a concept of the self which will make clear its interpersonal constituents; the following offers one example:

Each moral career, and behind this, each self, occurs within the confines of an institutional system, whether a social establishment such as a mental hospital or a complex of personal and professional relationships. The self, then, can be seen as something that resides in the arrangements prevailing in a social system for its members. The self in this sense is not a property of the person to whom it is attributed, but dwells rather in the pattern of social control that is exerted in connection with the person by himself and those around him. This special kind of institutional arrangement does not so much support the self as constitute it (*Asylums,* p. 168).

By moral career, Goffman seems to mean changes in the way a person perceives himself; in the essay from which this excerpt is taken, Goffman analyzes the moral career of mental patients. The essay is interesting not only because it so pointedly makes clear that a self is constituted—at least in part—by social arrangements, but because to some extent, Goffman intimates some dissatisfaction with this idea. Let us briefly review his argument in this essay in order to make this clear.

Goffman argues that one central theme in the experience of being a mental patient is the fluctuation and manipulation of the social arrangements which constitute the self, carried out—first by the staff and then by the patient—in such a way that the patient learns that a self can be arbitrarily constructed to fit any particular set of social arrangements. Goffman seems to argue that at first the patient takes his self for granted, without fully appreciating its dependence on social arrangements. Then he undergoes an experience—during the prepatient phase before he comes to the hospital—of seeing some of the social supports for his self erode; he sees people he thought of as friends and relatives helping to erode those social supports. He feels betrayed by these people, who often play an active role in getting him labeled a psychotic so that he will be hospitalized. Then, inside the hospital, he experiences a series of changes in the way he is treated as he moves from one ward to another, from one staff member to another. Unlike many of the changes which occur on the outside in real life, the changes inside the hospital seem relatively arbitrary to the patient. Once he grasps their arbitrariness, he has begun to feel and think that his own self can be changed easily; he learns to present a self which is appropriate for a given situation. Once that happens, he has become what Goffman calls morally loosened or morally fatigued (see *Asylums,* pp. 163-69). Once a person *feels* the way in which a self is constituted by more or less arbitrary social arrangements, then he has lost what we ordinarily refer to as a sense of morality. The word *feels* is emphasized because the patient's experience goes beyond an intellectual appreciation of the sort that could be gained from reading books—by reading some of Goffman's books for that matter.

Goffman states that when the mental patient has learned—deeply, feelingly, experientially—what he says throughout his books (that selves exist through presentations, that selves are constituted by social arrangements) then he has lost a sense of morality, or has become, in Goffman's term, morally loosened. The loosening consists in the patient's appreciation that there are no direct ties between oneself and the world; there are only signs mediating between the two, and those signs are susceptible to manipulation.

Ordinarily we express ourselves without thinking about this; Goffman states that mental patients often begin to see that there is no necessary connection between what one feels, what one expresses, and what one is taken for by others. These are the connections that are loosened.

This section on Goffman's views of self and society has dealt with two of his arguments: that a self arises from opposition to social pressures, and that a self is constituted by social arrangements. The easiest way of reconciling these two divergent views is to look back on our earlier discussion of the fragmented self: Goffman's view of the self divides it into parts each of which, at any given time, can take different positions or stances with regard to any given social pressure being placed on a person. One part of oneself accedes to the social pressure in some degree; another part refuses in some degree; this seems to be Goffman's image of us.

Ideas: Embarrassment. One of Goffman's recurrent themes is the strains that are created when one's appearances or presentations are not believed by others or are discredited by others. Thus Goffman writes of embarrassment, shame, losing face, and similar phenomena, all of which he analyzes as arising from a sense that one's presentation is not believed. Goffman discusses much of the ritual of daily life as designed to forestall a sense of embarrassment, to prevent one's losing face. He views social life as involving people who·cooperate to sustain certain definitions of various situations; we all continually take part in rituals and ceremonies toward this end.

CRITICAL EVALUATION OF GOFFMAN'S THOUGHT

1. Moral loosening.

Goffman's analysis of the experience of a mental patient involves what he calls moral loosening. By this, Goffman means that the patient obtains a vivid sense of how appearances can be manipulated to construct a self (a self for others: one which they will perceive and therefore think real). However, much of Goffman's writing seems directed toward demonstrating that this is a universal condition of life: the hidden sides of people (feelings, attitudes, etc.) are expressed by signs which are interpreted by others, and each of us must recognize that others may not interpret the signs correctly. Thus each of us is led into presenting signs in such a way that others will read us correctly; and having started down that road, we are all well on the way to becoming con men, callous and indifferent to issues of deception and misrepresentation. In this sense, Goffman argues that being a patient in a mental hospital offers an experiential education in the truth of what he says in his books. But why is this to be called moral loosening and moral fatigue?

By using these terms, Goffman seems to imply a criticism of his own point of view. There is other evidence that Goffman is made uneasy by his own ideas. Some of the evidence lies in his bizarre tone, already referred to. Some of the evidence lies in the contrast between his own certain confident tone and his content. His tone implies an author with abundant conviction, who is not lost in a quicksand of relativity. Contradictory evidence lies in the retrograde points he occasionally makes; sometimes Goffman offers an insight which undercuts much of his own general point of view, an insight which arises out of some moral scruple which is inconsistent with his general aim.

For example, one of Goffman's major points about mental hospitals is that the patient is quickly driven to an appreciation of the way in which what he says and does may be interpreted differently by the observing staff than the patient intended. The patient says, "I'm not crazy," and the staff nods and says, in effect, "See, you are crazy; the fact that you say you are not proves that you are." Or the patient screams with rage, and the staff nods and says "Inappropriate affect," since, in their view there is nothing to be enraged about. Discussing this point near the end of *Asylum,* Goffman says:

> In a psychiatric hospital, failure to be an easily manageable patient—failure, for example, to work or to be polite to staff—tends to be taken as evidence that one is not "ready" for liberty and that one has a need to submit to further treatment. The point is not that the hospital is a hateful place for patients but that for the patient to express hatred of it is to give evidence that his place in it is justified and that he is not yet ready to leave it. A systematic confusion between obedience to others and one's own personal adjustment is sponsored (*Asylums,* p. 385).

It is this last sentence that is interesting, since one wonders how—given Goffman's view of the relation between man and the society he lives in—such a simple contrast between obedience and personal adjustment is tenable. This contrast smacks of the conventional view of our society, wherein there are thought to be various independent people, each trying to gain some personal happiness on the one hand, and each on the other hand trying to get along with others. The conventional view plays down the interdependence of men, the extent to which one's own happiness is not an independent datum 'existing privately within one's own consciousness. This view is clearly not Goffman's, for the most part; yet occasionally he seems to express just that.

Goffman seems to argue that all of society is permeated by a systematic confusion between personal adjustment and obedience; and that, furthermore, this is no *confusion* at all, but rather the *reality* to which our conventional views about individual autonomy and liberty are inadequate. Most of the time Goffman seems to argue that it is our conventional views that are confusing, the views that elevate a contrast between obedience and personal autonomy into a revelation of reality. In fact, if one takes Goffman's books seriously, the distinction is untenable.

2. Authenticity.

Goffman's focus on the way we try to present a self in daily interaction while constantly taking precautions to make that presented self acceptable—or at least unobjectionable—to others, raises interesting questions when juxtaposed with the viewpoints generated by existential philosophy and contemporary humanistic psychology. Goffman himself seems aware that his point of view varies from that articulated by such writers as Sartre; for example, Goffman comments in a footnote that "This role of the witness in limiting what it is the individual can be has been stressed by Existentialists, who see it as a basic threat to individual freedom. See Jean-Paul Sartre . . ." (PS, p. 13). Goffman is noncommittal here; he does not say what he thinks of Sartre's position, but merely points out that Sartre's view differs from his own. But in another book there is a reference to Sartre which implies that Goffman thinks Sartre's view of these matters mistaken, or limited.

Goffman discusses ambiguity in social relationships. He offers an example of ambiguity, taken from Sartre, describing a woman's behavior with a man she has recently met. They talk, and all goes smoothly; but then the man takes her hand. She can withdraw it or enjoy the hand-holding; either way, she is changing the relationship, either by making clear that she does not welcome such intimacy, or that she does. Or she may try to do something in between, to leave her hand in his while acting as though it is not really there, or as though it is a thing divorced from her as she goes on talking. This last reaction is more ambiguous, of course. Goffman comments: "We could, following Sartre, moralistically call this 'bad faith' or could follow Bateson and call it something darker, but bad engineering it is not" (RP, p. 208).

Goffman implies that he regards such ambiguities differently from Sartre or Bateson; he argues throughout his books that such ambiguity is the essence of much of our social relations and cannot easily be done away with. Sartre's concept of bad faith roughly means saying one thing and feeling another, or not making clear what you feel or think. The reference to Bateson is presumably to his argument that much of schizophrenia arises out of confused communications, particularly the sort he calls a *double bind*. Sartre and Bateson can be interpreted as arguing that clearer, more honest communication would make all of us healthier. This, of course, is a prominent theme in much contemporary popular psychology—for example, the encounter-group school. Goffman's view is different; he believes that ambiguity and lack of clarity in communication preserves our social order (this is one argument), or enhances our ability to maintain our selves (another related argument). Self and society: they are fragile structures erected in part through what Goffman calls strategic tact (RP, p. 208), which requires being tentative in one's assertions and in one's reactions to others' assertions. This tentativeness in defining situations and relations can seem confusing: one does not know where one stands, perhaps; but without it, a lot of social life might disintegrate into brawling. And Goffman suggests further that not only would there be more fighting and less pleasure if this kind of tact were diminished, but also that what we think of as our selves emerges out of this constant exercise of social tact.

Perhaps the simplest way to present Goffman's view is that without a presentation of self, a self is not possible. The self does not really exist until presented; and the presentation of self immediately connects the self to the social matrix, since every presentation implicitly considers how others will react to the self presented. Further, one modifies that presentation to fit one's own sense of what others will tolerate or welcome; and if others will not tolerate one's presentation, one usually changes it. This argument is easy to grasp on the surface, but at a deeper level it is confusing. The confusion derives from our ordinary assumption that the self being presented is independent of the presentation. Goffman argues the opposite: the self is not independent of the presentation (the outward show); but if that is the case, how does the presentation get engineered? Who does the presenting? Goffman does not answer that question.

3. What is an individual, a self?

Minimally we are forced to a picture of a person, complicated because there is not only the executive capacity to present, to put on a show, but the sensory capacity to discern how others are reacting to that show, and an additional integrative capacity (connecting that sensory feedback into one's presentation). Moreover, there must be some *things* (not necessarily static), however elusive and tenuous, to be presented, which are to some extent dependent on the executive capacity and the presentation and others' reactions to the presentation, but also to some extent independent of these factors.

Where does this relatively complex picture leave us when we ask the existentialist questions about authenticity (the opposite of bad faith)? How can one be authentic in this kind of situation? Goffman never poses this question, of course. He operates on a plane of inquiry where the question of authenticity never arises. However, addressing the question to Goffman seems potentially fruitful, given our interest in how one conceptualizes the relationship between person, self, and society.

Much of the recent humanistic Third Force growth-potential movement psychology assumes that people can be authentic if they try. Being authentic means being who you are (rather than who other people want you to be); it means expressing feelings rather than hiding them; it means making the outward show (or *presentation,* in Goffman's term) conform as closely as possible with the inner reality. The assumption is that the inner reality is simple enough to be expressible, and that the inner reality (the true self) is not fragmented in a healthy person (although it may be in a "disturbed" person).

Goffman would not agree with these assumptions. His view of the inner self is that it is not simple, that it is fragmented whenever the self touches society; and further, that without society, there can be no self. Thus inner fragmentation is inevitable in his view. This is not necessarily to imply that people are going to be unhappy; fragmentation may not lead inevitably to unhappiness. Since the inner self is not simple, it is not expressible in one coherent gesture, although this is the dream that many of us pursue sometimes, searching for the one perfect gesture or act which will reveal us to everyone for what we really are.

The similarity between Goffman's portrayal of inevitably fragmented people, and Laing's portrait of selves which consist of a variety of internalizations of images of others coexisting in an uneasy juxtaposition is obvious. Both Goffman and Laing present a view of people who have the greatest difficulty knowing themselves and the greatest difficulty working out a harmonious integration of themselves. This is important to keep in mind in considering whether social institutions harm individual selves. In light of what Laing and Goffman have to say, can one conceive of a self which is not infiltrated by society? Can one imagine a completely harmonious and consistent self? This question is central, and we shall return to it.

Philip Slater has expressed ideas which seem similar to

some of Goffman's thinking. For example, in his fascinating study of training groups (T-groups), Slater argues as follows:

> Sociologists have long been aware that it is impossible to make any headway with the common sense notion that a group is an association of persons, but largely on the grounds that a group is "more" than the sum of its component individuals. It might be more productive to stress the fact that it is also a good deal less. Unless we are to remain utterly fixated on physical bodies, it is apparent that a group is not a collection of individuals at all but only of pieces of them. If all of an individual were bound up in a group, we could scarcely talk of an individual at all, nor of fears of or wishes for envelopment, since he would in fact be enveloped (Slater, *Microcosm*, p. 251).

Like Goffman, Slater says that if we can reasonably talk of a person's fear of being swallowed up by the group, then that person could be composed of parts one of which is already enveloped, and another of which fears that envelopment. Slater's analysis of groups in *Microcosm* is clearly heavily indebted to Freud, but Goffman has arrived at a similar analysis out of a different tradition. Whether their views are true or not we should rejoice because Goffman and Slater are engaged in a conceptual enterprise whose aim is a framework and an accompanying vocabulary for describing the relations between self and society. The framework that they struggle toward is interesting (a) because it is built (in both cases) on such meticulous observation of social interaction; (b) because although each has staked out a different territory for purposes of observation, each has made a similar analysis; and (c) because the conventional view, which leads to ready talk of the individual's conforming to society and being oppressed by society, does not fully explain what happens in social interactions. People do conform; oppression does occur; but the dynamics of each of these important events is not simple. As the most thoughtful analyses of the phenomena of oppression have argued, and as has already been discussed, one is not made free simply by getting rid of an outside oppressor; much of the oppression is already within oneself.

Thus Goffman's view of the self is of a divided entity; he completely ignores the difficult question of what integrative capacities or forces exist which hold the different parts together. How the different parts cohere is off his main topic, and he ignores it. Instead he focuses on brilliantly showing how social interaction encourages splitting of the self. He shows how one essential characteristic of what we ordinarily call the self is that it can take stands in different places at the same time; it can stand against itself, as it were.

4. Autonomy.

However there is an opposing theme in Goffman. Goffman argues that the self emerges in opposition to a surrounding social reality, but his argument does not fit together easily with his analysis of the self's being constituted in and by society. Although in his discussion of mental hospitals, he talks of the patients' attempts to preserve some sense of autonomy by resisting the social pressures of the institution, his analysis does not—on his own grounds—make sense. For one of his inescapable points is that each of us is caught up in society in myriad ways.

The best way to make sense of his different arguments on this score is to argue that there is no simple, pure society, but rather a loose conglomeration of social units, each impinging on each of us in a variety of ways. Each of us responds to each kind of social pressure, in one way or another; but never do we entirely accede to any social pressure; in a sense, we play one off against another. The positions we establish in different parts of the surrounding social reality each give us a different kind of strength, a capacity to resist pressures coming from the others. On a very simple level, if we have friends, job, and family, we can derive strength from each one sufficient to resist some of the blandishments of the others. Thus although we exist in and through the different social realities we inhabit, we are never entirely prisoner of any given one.

But talking of autonomy in this context does not make sense. One is not so much autonomous as multiply constituted, and thus to some degree resistant to any particular form of social pressure.

5. Difficulty in gaining knowledge of self, others, and interactions.

Another of Goffman's themes is that we have grave difficulty in gaining accurate knowledge of either what we are or of what others are, and what goes on between us. Part of the difficulty in his view is the covertness of many of the *crucial terms* of these phenomena. What is happening (either within us, within others, or between us) is often hidden and hard to discern.

But another part of our difficulty derives from complexity. Each of us is complicated in a number of ways: in the sense that we have different parts, to be sure, which do not fit together neatly, some of which are hidden and out of view. But complicated also in that we behave differently —and *are* different—in different situations, so that depending on the situation which confronts us, various parts of ourselves will be called forth and performed. A new situation will bring out a new part of us, perhaps hitherto unsuspected.

Goffman's focus is on the presentations we make, on how we define situations, on the outward show. But underneath this focus is his vision of the complexity of reality: the reality of self, of other, and of interaction. This of course is also part of his modern tone mentioned earlier. He shies away from reality in order to concentrate on the appearance, but as is fitting in one who has conceptual ambitions, who wants to piece things together and find the underlying connections, he has a powerful recurrent interest in the underlying reality. He sees the reality of people as complex, divided, partly submerged (or difficult of access), changing somewhat from situation to situation. These are all points to keep in mind as we continue.

Part of Goffman's concern with the difficulties of gaining knowledge about people can be seen in his preoccupation with deception, with pretense, with attempts to fool others (he keeps returning to accounts of spies who make a career out of fooling other people). He tries to help us cope with the problem of deception in other people and in ourselves. Usually he simply concludes that we do not need to be terribly concerned with deception, since all appearances are to some extent discrepant from reality. Here he either commits a conceptual error in lumping together cases of deception (where one knows one thing and says another) with cases of failure to tell the whole truth (one can probably never tell the whole truth about anything); or he expresses an essentially religiously tragic view of life (in picturing us as all more or less equally guilty at all times of deception, as being caught up in evil lies and morally loosened in spite of our best efforts to the contrary).

6. Ambiguity.

Goffman's analysis of the role of ambiguity in interpersonal relations is important. For if ambiguity or multiple meaning are seen as central to our relations with ourselves and others, then any simple insistence on the importance of being oneself or saying what one feels becomes more difficult. We shall now consider one of the foremost psychologists whose name has become identified with such a simple point of view, Carl Rogers. For Rogers's whole point of view is predicated on the assumption that one can be what one is; my argument will be that such a point of view is (a) difficult to reconcile with the important contributions made by Marcuse, Laing, and Goffman to our understanding of what people are like in their relations with one another; and (b) vitally linked with some of the social criticisms considered earlier. This is not a simple cause-and-effect connection; but both the Rogerian insistence on *being what you are* (along with the various encounter group and humanistic psychology manifestations) and the social criticisms arise from some deeply American belief in the sacredness of the individual and his or her opposition to the surrounding society. Let us consider first Rogers's thought and then its implications for the general argument of this book.

CHAPTER 6

Carl Rogers and Being Oneself

In a letter about education to *Commentary* some years ago, John Holt commented that ". . . most people define education as sculpture, making children what we want them to be. I and others . . . define it as gardening, helping children to grow and find what they want to be." This juxtaposition of metaphors is crucial for understanding much contemporary debate about the relation between people and any social institution. What is crucial about these metaphors is the simplicity of the distinction they attempt to establish: between putting children (and people) into a mold one has made, and simply helping them grow their own way. Using these metaphors to keep this distinction simple involves ignoring what many sculptors have said about their work as releasing the form "hidden within" the material. Likewise, one must also not think too hard about gardening, for most gardening is anything but letting things grow; one plants certain seeds and encourages them by weeding out other growing things. One fertilizes the soil;

144

one places sticks in the ground for the tomato plants to grow upon, and so on. Gardening is also a "making" (for example, Thalassa Cruso's *Making Things Grow*) and sculpting can be a helping.

But the point of the distinction is to contrast two modes of treating children (and people), and if we were to arrange contemporary thinkers on both sides of this distinction, undoubtedly Carl Rogers and most of what is called the humanistic psychology movement would go on the "gardening" side. Rogers believes wholeheartedly in letting people grow, and in helping them to grow the way they want to.

Carl Rogers is a psychotherapist whose ideas have drawn increasing attention during the past twenty to twenty-five years. He has worked all of his professional life as a therapist to help people; he is best known perhaps for what he calls his client-centered therapy, whose very name is designed to show an atheoretical stance. Rogers wants the focus of his therapy to be on the client (a word he prefers to the more conventional term "patient"), rather than on any theoretical framework which is intended to explain the client. Stating the major aim of his client-centered therapy is relatively easy: Rogers aims to provide a safe and secure atmosphere within which the client will be encouraged to grow as he or she wishes. Rogers's whole approach is very similar to Holt's notion expressed by the gardening metaphor; he thinks of himself as simply providing the right climate for healthy growth. In his own words:

> ... in my early professional years I was asking the question: How can I treat, or cure, or change this person? Now I would phrase the question this way: How can I provide a relationship which this person may use for his own personal growth? (p. 32) ... the individual has within himself the capacity and the tendency, latent if not evident, to move forward toward maturity. In a suitable psychological climate this tendency is released and becomes actual rather than potential (p. 35, from an essay "The Facilitation

of Personal Growth," in *On Becoming a Person*, pp. 31-38).

The tendencies toward healthy growth—in Rogers's view—come from within and flower given the right climate; in his own words, "... if I can supply a psychological amniotic fluid, forward movement of a constructive sort will occur" ("A Humanistic Conception of Man", p. 22). Here the metaphor of fetal development shows that he views himself as helping the client to give birth to or release the healthy self that is within.

Why does not the healthy self appear on its own? Rogers's answer is one common to the entire humanistic psychology movement: because one was not raised within a safe climate to begin with and does not live now within a healthy environment, one's growth has been stunted, thwarted, or misguided. And the bad environment which is responsible for unhealthy growth is variously identified as one lacking in acceptance, warmth, love, attention, respect, or other psychological nutrients deemed vital to healthy growth.

The humanistic psychology movement is a recent one in American psychology; it has become organized only during the past ten or fifteen years. Before 1960, although there were scattered psychologists espousing views which would later come to be called humanistic there was no real movement, except in a hidden rising swell of opinion and belief. The origin of this contemporary movement was in counteraction to the general dominance of the psychoanalytic and behaviorist theories in psychology during the period 1920-1960. Behaviorist theory was dominant in academic psychology; psychoanalytic thought was dominant in clinical psychology (among therapists); and although there were rival points of view, these two theoretical orientations were clearly the most powerful. Some psychologists always had objected to one or another aspect of these dominant theories; Gordon Allport's book *Becoming* (1955), is a concise articulation of some of the strands of thought which would later become the backbone of the humanistic psychology of the sixties and seventies. Carl Rogers has been a central figure in the rise of this movement and is perhaps its foremost living exponent.

What the humanistic psychologists have in common is a belief that the image of people provided by behaviorist and psychoanalytic theory is inadequate. One way of phrasing one part of their objection to the conventional images is to say that the notion of people as machines or animals does not adequately reflect human capacity for psychological growth. Thus the term *growth* has become one of the passwords of this new movement in psychology. Further, one of the central issues for this new kind of psychology revolves around defining what it is to be human; thus this new psychology has closer affinities with both philosophy and anthropology than conventional psychology has. Thus when Rogers talks of his client-centered therapy, he is expressing a concern with keeping the focus on the human being, which is common to much of what is called humanistic psychology.

BEING ONESELF

Rogers has always been concerned with helping people to be themselves. Recently he has become interested in encounter groups, which he sees as potent vehicles for beneficial change; they involve people in becoming themselves. Are not people ordinarily themselves? On the face of it, this may seem bizarre. After all, who else can one be? How can one be other than oneself? But as Laing has shown, one of the appealing legacies of Freud's psychoanalytic theory is a persuasive picture of how people come to be other than what they were at birth.

Freud's portrait of human development includes his vision of how people become severely conflicted and confused because of an innate lack of harmony within themselves (contradictory instincts in Freud's view), overlaid by further conflicts between outside people and inside wishes. These new conflicts become internalized in Freud's view; he uses several terms to refer to the process whereby a conflict between pressures inside one and pressures outside one becomes an internal conflict: *identification, incorporation,* and *internalization.* But Freud's picture of the developing human is of a being which is prey to external pressures by virtue of an enormous dependency at birth, and he shows that these external pressures become internalized as the human being develops and grows.

Laing and Rogers have both been impressed by this portrait of humanity given us by Freud. But whereas Laing often emphasizes the destructive effects of others on one's authentic self, Rogers optimistically emphasizes the ways in which we can each learn to deal with these destructive effects. Both believe that these destructive effects are not necessary; in this way they diverge markedly from Freud, who was rather consistently pessimistic on this particular issue. Freud was quite firm in insisting that some conflict is ineradicable; even if the conflict between the newborn and the outside world is reduced markedly, some external and internal conflict will remain.

Rogers ignores that part of Freudian theory which emphasizes innate internal conflict, and instead emphasizes ways in which people can, if given the proper environment of security and safety, learn to grow out of those conflicts engendered by abrasion between their own desires and those of others. Rogers portrays a being with its own desires which are often thwarted by others, and with an unfortunate development in childhood whereby the desires of others come to seem as important as his own. He attempts to show how one can, if helped by others, learn to disregard those pressures exerted on one from outside and live to fulfill those desires which truly come from within and are one's own.

Rogers makes the conventional distinction between the facade (the public mask, the outer self) and the inner real self (Goffman questions this distinction). Thus in his descriptions of encounter groups (in *On Encounter Groups*) Rogers argues that in encounter groups, people first show their mask, then slowly learn to drop the mask and reveal themselves as they truly are. The point of the encounter is that it helps them drop the mask and to be who they are. Be here can mean *feel* fully, and thus refer to intrapsychic awareness; but more often it means to show and express fully and thus refers to what goes on between people. The assumption is that what one *is* is simple enough so that one can *be* that; and, further, that what stops one from being what one is is a set of originally external and later internalized pressures and forces which one can question and throw off, given enough group support.

SELF-ACTUALIZATION

A key concept in the humanistic psychology movement is *self-actualization*, a term made popular by the late Abraham Maslow. Although Rogers does not use it, clearly his point of view can be readily connected with this term. It means fulfilling one's potential or living up to one's full capacities. Rogers thinks that very few of us do this, although all of us could if we had the right support from others, or the right attitude toward ourselves. What is required is more openness to one's own experience; one needs to listen to oneself, to hear and feel what is going on within, and then to live in accordance with it. People have inner needs which are constantly expressing themselves but being ignored by most of us. In large part this picture derives from Freud, who showed us how powerful the inner needs are which we are born with, and how powerful is our attempt to suppress what they tell us. But Rogers goes far beyond Freud in his belief that we can afford to express these inner needs; Rogers clearly believes that all these inner needs are potentially expressible, and he sees no reason to fear their release (as Freud might have).

As we have seen, Marcuse is impatient with this currently popular notion of self-actualization. Insofar as self-actualization is construed as "doing one's own thing" or concentrating most directly on one's own needs and desires and fulfillment, it potentially isolates one from other people, isolates one from society at large. Marcuse himself has a vision of an "authentic" existence which would allow free individual development that is nonetheless socially responsible, in some way connected with social processes. However, Marcuse's impatience with the concept of self-actualization may be misplaced, for as Maslow makes quite clear (see the preface to the first edition of *Towards a Psychology of Being*) the term self-actualization is not meant to have such selfish or self-centered connotations, but implies transcendence (Maslow, p. vi) of a sort which might please Marcuse.

OPTIMISM

One of the characteristic features of both Rogers's thinking and that of the American wing of the humanistic psychology movement in general [1] is that it is exceedingly optimistic. This optimism is reflected in a general neglect of topics such as dread, anxiety, guilt, and what might be called the whole tragic dimension of human living. Although such topics are mentioned, they are not central. The optimism is further reflected in the characteristic assumption that people can find authenticity through sociability; that one can find one's real self through being with others, even though at the same time other people are blamed for most of what has gone awry in one's own development previously. The nice things people can do for one another are stressed, and the nasty things are kept out of the central focus of attention. The emphasis on growth might be called optimistic; everyone can grow no matter how limiting the factors of his earlier development. Exceptions might be made here for severely retarded or emotionally disturbed people, where earlier damage might be ultimately irreparable; but by and large, the general assumption is that each of us can grow more and more continuously, we can each

1. There is also a European part of the humanistic psychology movement, called existential psychology, introduced in this country in part by Rollo May. In general, the existential psychologists are less optimistic; they stress the problematic aspects of living more than do the American humanistic psychologists. See, for example, Viktor Frankl.

change for the better. This is the same kind of optimism that underlies the whole therapy enterprise of course, but it is carried to greater lengths.

Optimism is also reflected in the insistence that we should each express what we feel and strive for what we desire; apparently our feelings, if expressed, will not be harmful to ourselves or others, and our needs can be gratified without pain to ourselves or others. Not much need be said about this now, but it is an important point to keep in mind.

Characteristic of Rogers's optimism is a section called "Man has the capacity for sound choice" from one of his articles.[2] In this section, he argues that people, if they are open to their experience, will make sound decisions. Rogers wants to convince us that despite the complexity of any situation (in which, for example, we are talking with someone we know) we can decide correctly what to say and do. The data of course which one has to consider are very complex: one's own needs, the other person's needs, one's memories of previous talks, one's perception of what one is saying, one's perception of what the other is saying, one's memories of what the other person meant the last time he said this, one's perception of how the other perceives oneself, etc. But in spite of the complexity, Rogers is sure we can consider all this and then decide correctly what to say and do. Rogers concedes occasional error, but thinks our error-correcting capacities are immense. All that is required is to be in touch with reality, so that when a mistake occurs, we shall immediately know it and remember it the next time we are in the same situation.

UNITY AND HARMONY

Rogers believes quite firmly that there are unity and harmony in each of us, in our feelings and behavior. He speaks of therapy as helping us to find that unity (*On*

2. "A Humanistic Conception of Man," pp. 28-29, in Glass and Staude.

Becoming a Person, pp. 113-14). There is a wholeness within us if we can only discover it and liberate it. How far this view of people is from the view we have been exploring in Laing and Goffman! Rogers is convinced that this wholeness needs only to be discovered or revealed, that it is not an arbitrary imposition on one's feelings, not a false convenience which one artificially imposes on himself.

EVALUATION OF ROGERS'S IDEAS

1. Being: knowledge or expression?

Is Rogers concerned more with people knowing what they themselves are like, or with their showing themselves to others as they really are: self-knowledge or expression of that self-knowledge? He makes abundantly clear (in *On Encounter Groups;* but see also *On Becoming a Person*) that one need not always act the way one feels; one should, as he says, have the choice, however, and one has the choice only insofar as one knows what he feels. This is straight Freudian psychoanalytic theory: the emphasis is on consciousness of one's own feelings. But in other places Rogers seems to say that one has a duty to *be* what one truly is, and *being* seems to involve *showing* (to others as well as oneself). This comes out rather clearly in the book on encounter groups. Here he often praises spontaneous expression of emotion. Expression means showing by words or facial expression or whatever, what one is feeling. Yet even while extolling this expressiveness, Rogers cautiously insists that one is always choosing how to act, and that one has the responsibility to recognize that one is choosing how to act. For example, he shows himself in a difficult situation in an encounter group wondering what to do. This kind of wondering is rather far removed from spontaneity in the orthodox sense. He does not present clearly how the highly valued spontaneity ("spontaneity is the most precious and elusive element I know," *On Encounter Groups,* p. 57) is related to the clear emphasis on choice revealed in the following:

If one can only be *aware* of all the complexity of his feelings in any given moment—if one is listening to oneself adequately—then it is possible to *choose* to express attitudes which are strong and persistent, or not to express them at this time if that seems highly inappropriate. (*On Encounter Groups*, p. 53, author's italics)

This is important: worry about what is appropriate seems exemplary of the kind of social self (the public mask, in Rogers's own phrase) which Rogers seems at times to think so confining, so productive of bad feelings both in the person living the social self and in those around him. Putting this discussion together with what has been said earlier about Marcuse, one can see that both Rogers and Marcuse have a vision of a mode of being (of living) which would involve great fidelity to what is within one, yet both think this mode of being must be constrained by some grasp of what is outside one, what others are feeling, what others need. But of course, on Rogers's analysis, one reason people have problems knowing what they want to do is that they are attuned to what others want. So many of Rogers's examples, of how one adopts a facade or how one finds oneself doing things which are not enjoyable, are the archetypal examples of people feeling pressured into doing something because someone else wants it done. One feels the pressure because one is attuned to other's feelings and desires. And Rogers says, of the kind of self he thinks a person will become if he goes through successful therapy or a successful encounter group experience, that this new self is moving away from meeting others' expectations, away from doing what one ought to do (*On Becoming a Person*, Chapter 8).

So there is a fundamental lack of clarity here in Rogers's position. But he is very clear in stating his belief that people can learn to be what they truly are. The question is whether this involves a radical emancipation from society, or a radical submersion in society, or—somehow—both simultaneously. Paradoxically, Roger's advocation of the encounter group amounts to arguing that one can learn to

become free of the unwanted pressures of others by being
with others. Rogers may see two sets of others: one set
bound up in anxiety-provoking situations, forcing you to do
things by exerting pressures on you which you have difficulty resisting; the second set bound up in an environment
of safety and security (in the encounter group). Of course, in
addition to the conceptual and experiential mysteries (How
is one to be spontaneous while thinking about what is
appropriate? How is one to know which of those many
feelings bubbling around inside oneself are truly one's own
and which are incorporated from one's contacts with others?), there is the mystery of why it is that people are so
awful to one another ordinarily and yet so helpful to one
another in an encounter group.

2. Freedom from constraint.

The main thrust of Rogers's thinking is congruent with
an important theme in American culture; the whole encounter group movement is popular in part because its
ideology fits in so well with typically American thinking—the old American obsession with getting free of alien
social pressures. Freedom to do what one wants: that is part
of the American dream. Desire for freedom led many people to America originally; it led many more to go west while
that promised freedom; and it leads Americans today to
bewail the pressures of conformity and to seek liberation
from social pressures. Doing one's own thing: that has been
an American need for a long time.

Rogers does not portray himself as deriving from an
American cultural tradition, but he does put an important
passage from Emerson at the front of his *Client-Centered
Therapy*. Rogers quotes Emerson as follows:

> We mark with light in the memory the few interviews
> we have had, in the dreary years of routine and of sin,
> with souls that made our souls wiser; that spoke what
> we thought; that told us what we knew; that gave us
> leave to be what we inly were. (Emerson, "Divinity
> School Address," 1838)

The crucial phrase is the last: "leave to be what we inly were." Emerson implies that some people prevent us from being what we really are, and others help us to be what we are. This is Rogers's notion, too. But how do we know what we are?

Emerson is interesting because he fits so squarely within one important American tradition, one which Quentin Anderson refers to as *the flight from culture* (*The Imperial Self*, p. 3) or as the development of an imperial self. Anderson shows us Emerson discussing the importance of the individual man and the irrelevance of society to the free development of the individual. Anderson underscores the attack on society implicit in so much of Emerson's insistence on self-reliance, on the importance of the self. Henry James and Walt Whitman are discussed in the same light:

> James is unlike Emerson and Whitman in that he admits and even brilliantly describes a various and voluminous world. But he is no less rigorous than they in making it submit to his own imaginative order. All three imaginations are so commanding, tend so much to incorporation, that we may properly speak of them as performing a function for their possessors analogous to that of a religion in other men. In all three the compelling character of history, generational order, places and things leaches out, tends to disappear (Anderson, p. 223).

This last is the point: that generational order tends to disappear; the fantasy is of a self unhooked from all determination by external contingency. One is not forced to be a bricklayer simply because one's father was; and in fact, what one's father is and was has no connection (here) with what oneself is. One is free of one's father; that is the appealing fantasy in Emerson, Anderson argues; and that is perhaps one part of the appeal in the current vogue of liberation through group meetings. One becomes free of the hangups foisted upon one by one's parents, and the disdain for one's parents is connected with the non-familiar attack on the nuclear family. The family is despised for restricting one's freedom. The vision is of a way of life where there are no restrictions, or so it seems. Remember our consideration of Marcuse's vision of a better world in which all constraint has dwindled to a bare vanishing point; in this respect, Marcuse is part of this general *Zeitgeist* as well. Of course, in most writers, as in Rogers, there is some tempering of this attitude by a recognition that, at times, one must pay attention to forces outside; one must think about what is appropriate, what one should do in a given situation depending on what others in the situation are feeling and wanting.

The popularity of encounter and sensitivity-training groups is an interesting phenomenon; Kurt Back's account of it (in his recent *Beyond Words*) is valuable, but an interesting light would be cast on the whole group phenomenon if it were considered in conjunction with other strands of American culture. In particular, American literature can be seen as embodying themes which resonate throughout the group movement. In fact, Poirier's book on American literature (*A World Elsewhere*) together with that by Anderson enable one to make a certain sense of this proliferation of groups.

Poirier discusses how so much of American literature can be understood as an attempt to build one's own world, away from the confining social world we all ordinarily inhabit. He refers to Thoreau: "Walden is only one of the examples of something like an obsession in American literature with plans and efforts to build houses, to appropriate space to one's desires, perhaps to inaugurate therein a dynasty that shapes time to the dimensions of personal and familial history" (p. 17). He argues further that ". . . Salinger's Holden Caulfield is a merely stock character enacting the American hero's effort, more significantly illustrated by Isabel Archer, to express the natural self rather than merely to represent in speech and manner, some preordained social type" (p. 27). And, more generally still, Poirier points to ". . . the tension of bringing into conjunction the environment of nakedness, where there is no encumbrance to the expression of the true inner self, and the environment of costume, of outer space occupied by society and its fabrications" (p. 30). Although Poirier's book examines American literature, this last passage can be seen as a description of a portion of the underlying dynamics of contemporary encounter groups: there is a tension between the desire to be rid of all encumbrances to the expression of the true inner self, and the opposing desire to do this in a social space (in a group, that is). America may be particularly hospitable to fantasies of complete individual freedom in a social context; this would help to explain why encounter groups are particularly popular here.

3. The potentials of human beings.

One of Rogers's central points is that people ought to fulfill their own potential. He assumes that each of us has potentials hidden within us which need some help to find release and expression. He further assumes that these potentials will do some good if released, not just for the one releasing them, but for others; and that these potentials are somehow more one's own than the behavior which ordinarily characterizes one, behavior which is more attuned to the need for *masks*: behavior which owes more to social pressures than to one's own needs.

It is this last assumption which seems most dubious; constructing a plausible argument to show exactly how these hidden potentials are peculiarly one's own would be difficult. Certainly the way in which Rogers usually makes this point is not sufficient. Usually he simply posits a young adult who feels forced into doing something—working in a bank because his father wants him to work there—but who really wants to play the piano. Rogers assumes that playing the piano is more peculiarly this man's own behavior than working in the bank. However, one might object that neither the piano playing nor the bank working would occur in a different social-cultural context: both desires and behaviors derive to some degree from the culture, albeit from different aspects of it.

Another problem with Rogers's analysis is that each of us has many potentials, most of which are doomed to be unrealized, given the finiteness of life. We have limited time and energy. If one wants to be a very good pianist, then one must devote time and effort to piano playing, which necessarily eliminates other activities. One must choose which potentials to realize, and such choices are always hedged in by the awareness of the exclusion of other desires. European existentialist psychologists emphasize this whole topic much more than do Rogers, Maslow, or the American humanistic psychologists.

Then there is the problem of knowing which potentials, among the many one can discern dimly within, are most important. Here also the existential psychologists will emphasize the need for choice, for fulfilling one potential rather than another; whereas the American humanistic psychologists like Rogers will characteristically talk about how one will just *know* which potential needs to be gratified first, which later, and so forth. Rogers assumes that if one is open to his experience, if one is aware of what he is experiencing, one will know with great confidence not only how to behave at any given point, but how to organize his life, how to live in the broadest sense.

John Seeley makes the same point from another point of view. In discussing psychotherapy, he argues that the therapist helps the patient to see certain things as more real and more important than others:

> . . . the psychotherapist appeals from what is patent in his patient to what is latent; he interferes, he intervenes, and his intervention involves discrimination. (There is nothing virtuous or desirable in something merely because it is latent.) From among latent potentialities, he selects; and he selects in terms of an implicit agreement that he and the patient share, an agreement that is the unspoken social contract that combines the two into a society in some full sense. . . .
> (*The Americanization of the Unconscious,* pp. 123-24)

The crucial phrase here is the following: "from among la-

tent potentialities, he selects" for he argues as I have that
there are many potentials in each of us from which we must
choose. How to choose? In accordance with which set of
values?

A similar vantage point can be gained on this discussion
from the point of view of some modern literature. For
example, the literary critic Wylie Sypher comments, in discussing the work of André Gide: "Early in the twentieth
century Gide . . . remarked that the self is capable of anything. He implied that the romantic quest for sincerity—the
finding of the real self—is a ridiculous venture. For as he
discovered, if you remove the pressure of the usual codes
even for an instant, we are capable of every sort of irrational,
unexpected act . . ." (*Loss of the Self in Modern Literature
and Art*, p. 64). Gide was European, and so are most of the
archetypical modern writers (Kafka, Joyce, etc.). The emphasis here, which I shall return to in the final chapter, is on
social pressures which help keep the irrational side of each
of us under control; or on social pressures which help us
choose among a large number of internal desires all of which
want gratification. This kind of preoccupation, so natural to
Freudian thought, is foreign to Carl Rogers.

An interesting argument related to the constrast between
the typically American exhortation to everyone to fulfill his
potentials and the European existentialist emphasis on the
constant need for choice (for choosing which potential to
fulfill) is provided by recently emerging futurologists, a
small army of people who are interested in looking into the
future. The humanistic psychologists are linked with the
futurologists in their concern about the directions in which
people are moving. Carl Rogers has even written an article
called "Interpersonal Relationships: USA 2000" [3]

3. An organization called The World Future Society in Washington
has been putting out a magazine called *The Futurist* for about ten years
now. A lot of futurology consists of forecasting trends, as in all the
proliferating studies of "The Year 2000," which try to show what life in
America will be like in the year 2000. But some of the futurology writing
is frankly normative: it posits certain values as ideal, and then shows us
how we can move toward fulfilling them in the future. Theobald's book
has a substantial bibliography of works in this field.

Writers in this field commonly argue that the development of technology has, for the first time, truly enabled man to make his own future—not only the future of the world he lives in but the future of his own nature, his own evolution. As Willis Harmon argues in an interesting collection of essays put together by Robert Theobald:

> ... the present point in the history of man may well, when viewed in retrospect by some future generation, appear as a relatively sudden cultural step. The portentous impact of the new technology is the heady yet sobering realization that we have the future in our hands, that man recognizes his role as, to use Julian Huxley's phrase, "a trustee of evolution on this earth." The new man, "homo progressivus" in Teilhard de Chardin's words, is described by Lancelot Law Whyte as "unitary man," by Lewis Mumford as the "new person," and by Henry A. Murray as an "ally of the future." The challenge of our time is whether we make "the step to man" or our Faustian powers prove our undoing and the whole vast machine goes off the track through the strains of internecine conflict and degradation of the environment (Harmon, p. 186).

Here is an American version of the existential emphasis on choice, but the need for choice is seen not as an essential constituent of living, of being, but as a result of technological advances over the past two centuries. The argument is very similar to that of Marcuse: technological capability has recently freed people from the chains of necessity. The spirit animating this vision is truly optimistic: people are portrayed as becoming totally different from what they have been hitherto, becoming new people, evolving beyond anything known before. This attitude is, perhaps, an American reworking of the European existential emphasis on the necessity of choice; in the version provided by Harmon, choice is not a necessity nor a burden, but a glorious opportunity to ascend to higher levels of being.

This position moves from an old view of technology as

freeing people, as benefiting people. The contemporary wave of futurologists and humanistic psychologists are perhaps linked together, then, in their optimism about the eventual results of freeing people to fulfill their potentials. This is not to say that the humanistic psychologists are agreed with the futurologists on every point; for example, the humanistic psychologists typically are more skeptical about the benefits of technology, arguing that it tends to mechanize human relations, to impersonalize social intercourse.

4. The unity of the self.

Rogers thinks that unified selves are within us, waiting to be discovered and liberated. This implicitly denies the importance of the many forces tending toward fragmentation. For example, Goffman stresses the way in which playing different roles involves the forging of different selves (or different parts of our self). Rogers would argue instead that this should not happen; we should strive for consistency, we should strive to be the same in all situations, and this ideal is held up as embodying honesty, candor, even reality. Rogers talks of being real, and that means being oneself regardless of the external situation. However, Rogers also recognizes that the feelings we each have fluctuate from moment to moment; and he also recognizes that of many feelings we have, only a few will be expressed at any given time. He even briefly discusses the necessity of choosing which ones to express and when to express them. This kind of choosing would seem to imply a division within the self, at least into two parts: the feelings on the one hand, and that part of us which decides which to express, and when and how. But Rogers does not clarify this position any further. One way might be to posit unity as an ideal toward which we should each strive, but Rogers does not appear to take this point of view.

A friendly critic, reading this passage, pointed out that differentiation and opposition (within a person's psychological organization) do not in themselves imply any lack of unity. As he put it, "homogeneity is not a criterion of unity." [4] Of course, unity does not require homogeneity; this seems obvious once it is said. Rogers's emphasis on the importance of expressing ourselves, and on being real and being ourselves, does not necessarily imply that we are simple and homogeneous. However, Rogers is a psychological theorist who emphasizes simplicity, and who deemphasizes the complexities of internal conflict; this is the point which must be emphasized.

To some extent, the problem resides in differences in ways of characterizing human complexity. We can either say of a person that he is complicated (leaving up in the air the question of whether that is good or bad), or that he is ambivalent or fragmented or conflicted (implying that he is not altogether healthy, psychologically). Necessary here is a conception of human complexity which (a) allows for psychological differentiation, and yet also (b) makes clear which differentiation is good and healthy (because part of an organized whole for example) and which is unhealthy (not organized, not held together). All of this is very difficult, at present, especially given the tendency of conventional psychological thinking to posit an integrating context (the personality we often call it) for *all* individual behavior, feeling, mood, and attitudes. But Rogers does not help make the task easier when he stresses such simplistic slogans as "be who you are" and "be real." These slogans imply an individual harmony and integration which, taken as an ideal, may make sense, but taken as a description of ordinary human reality leaves something to be desired.

5. Relations with others.

Perhaps the weakest point of Rogers's analysis of the human situation is the way he deals with relationships between people. He discusses them in at least three contexts: in therapy, between therapist and client; in encounter groups, among the participants; and in marriages, between the partners. He has written at least one book about each of

4. Isidor Chein, in a letter to the author.

these topics.[5] In all these books, Rogers espouses the conviction that if each of us is real and strives to become what he truly is, the group will prosper. This is a psychological version of Adam Smith's economics. Both theories hold that if one takes care of oneself, the group as a whole will inevitably benefit. What is interesting is that Rogers is *not* the Adam Smith of psychology. In fact, although there are parts of his writing which sound like this, he is always careful—if taken on the whole and in context—to make clear that each of us must be considerate of others. Each of us must respect others. In fact, respect for others is the cornerstone of his therapeutic method; the therapist heals because he respects his client, because he has a careful regard for the client. But the problem is to reconcile this regard for the other with being who one truly is. How can one be the person one really is while caring for others? If others' needs are important, and if I need to be considerate of them, then my needs are inextricably bound up with theirs. And it is the inextricable intermingling of one person's needs with others' which most of Rogers's theory fails to elucidate.

In a very similar way, Maslow's theories of self-actualization fail to make clear the interpersonal dimension of self and needs. For this reason, both Rogers and Maslow are liable to misinterpretation; each attract followers whom they would each disown. Rogers expresses his uneasiness with some of those who have taken up with the encounter group movement, and Maslow similarly expresses uneasiness with some of the interpretations given his concept of self-actualization. Yet in a very important way, each man's thoughts almost inevitably call forth such misinterpretations, such followers. For much of Rogers's thinking (and that of the entire humanistic psychology movement) concentrates far too heavily on the duties one owes oneself and one's own needs and potentials, at the expense of making clear where these duties run into the needs of others.

5. *Client-Centered Therapy; On Encounter Groups;* and *Becoming Partners.*

Rogers's book on marriage *(Becoming Partners)* states that it is possible for two people each to be who they are and yet live in harmony with each other, although he admits this is no easy task. Similarly, he often says that entire societies can live in peace and harmony if only people learn to respect each other's individuality. But all this is much easier said than done; and, more importantly, Rogers fails to offer any help with the sticky question of exactly how one works out these connections between one's own needs and the needs of others, between what one owes himself and what one owes others.

One way of viewing Rogers's quandary is simply to point out that much of his thinking about what goes wrong with people derives quite directly from Freud. And insofar as Freud's therapy and theory are primarily individualistic, so is Rogers individualistic. Rogers's model of human pain and trouble is essentially Freudian: he thinks our trouble is that we repress feelings, we ignore parts of our experience, we shut off one part of our thought from another part. He argues that this repression and internal closing-off lead to pain and suffering within each of us, and, by implication, within the society at large. He finds that the way for each of us to improve (to become healthier) is to cease this internal blocking and repression; he thinks a good therapist, by being real and genuine (that is, by being his experience, by providing a model of one who is internally integrated, who does not shut off aspects of his experience), will help the client to become real and genuine; and that once we are real, we will be better off. This analysis ignores what Freud ignored: the social dimension of much of our suffering. This is too remorselessly psychological a vision of human suffering. Of course, that such a vision should flow from a man who has done mainly individual therapy for over thirty years is not surprising. But there are social dimensions of suffering which this picture slights.

Rogers's belief that people can help one another implies a social dimension to his thought (equally true of Freud). And if there is one point that is central to Rogers's writing over the past several decades, it is that we can indeed help each other: in therapy, in encounter groups, in our marriages, in society in general. But the extent of his helping us gain a conceptual understanding of how people relate to society does not go much beyond his arguing that the therapist can provide a model to the client (which the client can imitate, as it were); or that the therapist can create a safe climate for the client in which the client can grow; or that being psychologically real is contagious (if I am real, if I experience my feelings, then I will automatically be helping you to be more real). And even this kind of analysis falters when it fails to make explicit the social dimension of this process: Rogers is never clear about how much of the process of being real involves expression and communication with the other. Sometimes he seems to say that we must bring our expression into line with our feelings; this begins to sound like Goffman talking about constructing outer appearances which will be congruent with one or another impression we want to convey. At other times Rogers talks of simply being aware of one's feelings, and the issue of whether one is communicating them to others is mentioned as a separate issue, not necessarily connected with the first.

Rogers makes very clear that even in the humanistic psychology movement, which has arisen out of a dissatisfaction with both psychoanalytic and behaviorist thought, there is no clear thrust toward a more truly social psychology. There is perhaps a different tone than is found in Freud; but there is no truly new conceptual achievement so far, certainly none that would help us understand better the kinds of connections we are hoping to elucidate. We had to consider Rogers's thought because if he were persuasive in his argument that people have a self which they ought to actualize, or that each of us has a unified self within, then he would have effectively demonstrated that the kind of social-psychological theory of people which is needed would be limited to one which specifies the social influences on the components of the inner self. Such a theory of course already exists; in fact, there are any number which emphasize how social processes influence the formation of components of the self (e.g. Freud's theory of how the superego is formed). However, our argument is that this sort of limited social-psychological theory of personality does not clarify the extent and degree to which the people's needs, desires, thoughts, and motives have a continuously social context, and find their very existence within a social field which is broader than the body of the person whom we say has the feelings and motives. With Rogers's theory, we might still need a social psychology of relations between these unified separate autonomous selves, or of the origins of the self, but we would not need a social-psychological theory of the present and ongoing self.

Thus we find that Rogers's theory does not move us very far in the direction we want to go. We can move on now to consider other approaches to social-psychological theorizing which may help us to see at least some of the complexities involved in formulating social-psychological theory.

CHAPTER 7

Kenneth Burke
and Thomas Schelling:
Toward a
Relevant Conceptual Structure

From considering some of the ambitions of psychologists—to develop a theory which would integrate sociology and psychology, as in Keniston; or to erect a relevant conceptual structure which would help us reorder society so that people would be happier, as in Skinner—I have examined some of the criticisms of our social institutions, and considered various writers whose thinking contains the beginnings of an understanding of how incredibly complicated the connections between individual and society actually are. The *complexity* of these connections undercuts any easy analyses about conflict between the individual and society. One cannot, in the light of these theoretical viewpoints, talk simply about the individual rebelling against society, or about the society forcing the individual to conform. For the individual and the society are caught up in each other to an extent greater than such analyses imply.

I have also pointed out how the theoretical developments we have been considering make difficult any simple formulation of ideas about personal authenticity. There may be some realm of authentic human existence, but it is apparently not to be found in isolation from sociability. Let us turn to the work of two thinkers who have points of view which might be helpful in working out a genuine social psychology which, while having respect for empirical research, will also have some conceptual power. These writers are Kenneth Burke and Thomas Schelling.

Each of these writers has written extensively; my aim is not a thorough survey of their writing, but a very selective sampling of their ideas which are pertinent to psychology in general and to social-psychological issues in particular. Such work is relevant to psychology even though it is done by nonpsychologists. Psychology has won the war of independence; its former dependence on other fields such as philosophy, sociology, and physiology has vanished. But along with the dependence on these other fields went the connections between psychology and the humanities and social sciences. In general, psychologists are not accustomed to consulting people outside their field, except where interdisciplinary research is encouraged by institutional structures. Usually psychologists are content to refer only to one another in their articles and books; and there is little awareness of the help available in philosophy, literary criticism, and even the closely allied fields of sociology and anthropology. This lack of connection may be a general characteristic of the intellectual disciplines today, but it seems particularly pronounced in psychology. My consideration of Burke and Schelling is meant in part to convey appreciation for what writers in other fields have to offer psychologists, especially in difficult questions of general theory.

KENNETH BURKE

Kenneth Burke is a fascinating, exciting writer who deserves to be better known among psychologists. He is not well known partly perhaps because he is primarily identified as a literary critic, and psychologists have—at least recently in this country—not been accustomed to turning to literary criticism in order to augment their psychological understanding. Perhaps he is not so well known as he might be because of his difficult style: his thinking is not easy to penetrate, and his method of exposition is rather rambling and free-associative, by conventional standards.

BURKE'S RELEVANCE FOR PSYCHOLOGY

At least five books have been written about Burke, and numerous articles, many of the best of which have been collected into one volume [1]; but in all this, there is very little for the psychologist. Very little of it explicitly and clearly deals with that part of Burke's work which is most obviously relevant to psychology. Nonetheless, Burke has obtained some recognition for the quality and importance of his writings on psychological themes; for example, Stanley Hyman, the literary critic, has pointed out the importance of Burke's social psychological theories (Hyman, p. 329); and Hugh D. Duncan, the sociologist, has written at least two books in which Burke's ideas are used extensively.[2] Some of Burke's works have been favorably reviewed by sociologists and psychologists. Louis Wirth says of Burke's *Permanence and Change*: "This is a book to put some of the authors and publishers of sociological textbooks to shame. It contains more sound substance than any text on social psychology with which the reviewer is familiar" (Wirth, p. 102).

Although Duncan and other sociologists as well have used Burke's ideas for their own purposes; and although numerous literary critics have, in writing about Burke's literary criticism, pointed out the pertinence of his psychological observations, no one has tried to discuss selectively that part of Burke's thinking which is directly pertinent to social psychology. This has struck many of Burke's admirers

1. See G. Knox: *Critical Moments;* M. Brown: *Kenneth Burke;* A. P. Frank: *Kenneth Burke;* V. Holland: *Counterpoint;* W. Rueckert: *Kenneth Burke and the Drama of Human Relations;* and W. Rueckert, ed.: *Critical Responses to Kenneth Burke.*

2. See *Communication and Social Order* and *Language and Literature in Society.*

with surprise. For example, Rueckert comments on an essay
by Harry Slochower:

> So far as I know, this is one of the few essays on Burke
> by someone trained (formally or otherwise) in psy-
> chology. Erving Goffman was later to make extensive
> use of Burke in his book *The Presentation of Self in
> Everyday Life* but he never wrote directly about him.
> It seems unfortunate, given Burke's really profound
> debt to Freud, Jung, and psychology in general, that
> we have never had the benefit of work on Burke by
> experts in this field (Rueckert, *Critical Responses*, p.
> 136).

What in Burke's thought would seem interesting to psychologists? Examine his comment on Freud (typically
tossed off in a footnote; Burke often has difficulty in deciding what to put in the body of his work and what to restrict
to his footnotes, and he makes many interesting points in
footnotes):

> It is wrong, I think, to consider Freud's general picture
> as that of an individual psychology. Adler's start from
> the concept of ego compensation fits this description
> par excellence. But Freud's is a family psychology. He
> has offered a critique of the family, though it is the
> family of a neo-patriarch. It is interesting to watch
> Freud, in his *Group Psychology and the Analysis of
> the Ego*, frankly shifting between the primacy of group
> psychology and the primacy of individual psychology,
> changing his mind as he debates with himself in public
> and leaves in its pages the record of his fluctuations,
> frankly stated as such. Finally he compromises by
> leaving both, drawing individual psychology from the
> role of the monopolistic father, and group psychology
> from the roles of the sons, deprived of sexual gratifi-
> cation by the monopolistic father, and banded to-
> gether for their mutual benefit. But note that the
> whole picture is that of a family albeit of a family in

which the woman is a mere passive object of male
wealth (PLF, pp. 233-34). [3]

Burke's point needs no comment, and Burke is only one
among many who have pointed out the subsidiary position
that women occupy in Freud's theory. However, Burke's
point—made in the thirties—that Freud's theory is a family
psychology, does deserve special comment. While admit-
ting that Freud's theory places a large emphasis on individual psychology (obvious in the analytic therapy which
Freud developed, in which people are treated individually)
Burke draws to our attention the extent to which an emphasis on the family is inherent in Freud's thinking. Although this is not nearly as interesting a point today as it
was forty years ago, his statement still has some shock value;
it seems paradoxical, unusual, because we have become so
accustomed to thinking of Freud's psychology as of the
individual. When Burke draws our attention to it, of course
we recognize that the Oedipal complex, for example, develops only within a familial context. We recognize that in
his case histories, Freud inevitably discusses the parents
(and brothers and sisters) of his patients. We recognize
that Freud again and again elaborates concepts such as identification, which assume a close connection between an
individual and his family (particularly his parents, or the
parental substitutes). When Burke draws our attention to
it, we can more easily see that the current family therapies
have grown out of Freudian theory.

In the passage quoted, Burke also states that Freud
offered a critique of the family. This observation contains
enough truth (although it is not wholly accurate) to help us
see how many contemporary psychoanalysts (such as Laing
and his co-workers) who started from a psychoanalytic
training and a familiarity with Freudian thinking, have
managed to work out a (rather violent) critique of the
family. Burke helps us see that Laing, in his critique of the

3. PLF: *The Philosophy of Literary Form.*

family and society, is not departing so far from Freud's thinking as we are sometimes told.

Burke is relevant for psychologists not only because he has read and thought about and manages to use Freud in penetrating ways, but also because he has obviously thought about some of the central dilemmas in contemporary psychology: behaviorism and its implications for our conceptions of what it is to be a man; the related issue of motivation; the relationships between individual acts and their social context. Further, one of his central topics is the role of communication and language in social relations. Finally, Burke argues effectively for the relevance of literature to the understanding of people—an idea that needs arguing in American psychology today, although Freud was a psychologist who needed no convincing on that score. Freud's use of literature in the development and illustration of his ideas seems to be one aspect of his thought which has not taken hold here in America, despite his tremendous influence.

BURKE'S TONE AND STYLE

Why have psychologists not read Kenneth Burke more extensively? First, he is identified generally as a literary critic and not as a psychologist; literature is not conceived by most psychologists as relevant for their work as professional psychologists, although there are exceptions.[4] But he is not seen as someone with something relevant to say for psychologists because of his identity as a literary critic, and his writing style is difficult to penetrate.

Adverse comments on Burke's style or method of presenting his ideas have been numerous. Burke tends to free-associate considerably, and when one idea reminds him of another—as is so often the case—he usually goes on to the second idea, whether or not the connection between it and

4. For example, Henry Murray, the psychologist at Harvard who is known for his interest in both personality theory and Herman Melville (and much else as well).

the first idea is clear to the reader. Burke does this so freely because he thinks that everything is related. So he does not object to bewildering the reader. He seems to be saying, "Well, following me is no harder than following most connections; the world is a very confusing place, to be sure, in which everything runs together quite a bit more than it does in my writing." One adverse comment on this characteristic of Burke's style may be representative: "This sort of thing undoubtedly dazzles one's admiration for dialectical acrobatics, but one shudders for literary criticism at the prospect of such equipment out of control" (Knox, p. 67).

Another important objection to Burke's writing is contained in the following:

> Burke's work . . . is single-voiced; as complex as it is, it is monotonal. Nor does Burke listen very carefully to himself. One has no sense in his work of the constant revision that accompanies dialectical writing (M. Brown, pp. 13-14).

Burke's "monotonal" writing means it is hard to read; one can pick up any of his books or essays and begin at almost any point without any greater sense that something has been skipped, than if one had begun at the beginning. What makes this difficult is the feeling of not getting anywhere.

BURKE'S THOUGHT

Burke certainly began with an interest in literature and its relations to life. His writings reveal the strong influence of both Marx and Freud. He seems to have become fascinated by the way in which different theories account for facts, and much of his recent works resembles what is usually called intellectual history; he shows how different theories grow out of each other and are related. However, his interest in literature is still great, and he continues to write literary criticism.

1. Literature and strategic naming.

In discussing Burke's interest in literature and life, I shall gradually enter into a consideration of his concern with communication and its role in social relations. In an essay called "Literature as Equipment for Living" (PLF, pp. 253-62) Burke states that literary works attempt to describe situations which are recurrent and important in a given social structure. If a situation arises often, people will try to talk about it; and one function of literature is to provide a way of talking—through a poem, novel, play, or whatever —about an interesting recurrent situation. As Burke says:

> A work like *Madame Bovary* (or the homely American translation, *Babbitt*) is the strategic naming of a situation. It singles out a pattern of experience that is sufficiently representative of our social structure, that recurs sufficiently often *mutatis mutandis,* for people to "need a word for it" and to adopt an attitude towards it (PLF, p. 259).

And after the novel is written, we will use the novel as a way of describing people: e.g., we will refer to someone as a Bovary or a Babbitt if we have read the novels and they have entered into our imagination.

In the above passage Burke talks of a "strategic naming," by which he means that any work of literature embodies not just a description of an event or series of events or people, but also implicitly takes an attitude toward those events or people. A strategic naming is a way of describing something that helps us cope with life. To give a simple illustration: Burke discusses proverbs such as "The sun does not shine on both sides of the hedge at once" and "He is not poor that hath little, but he that desireth much" as designed for consolation. They are verbal formulae which, when summoned to mind, may console us in a difficult situation. Burke goes on to say:

> Proverbs are strategies for dealing with situations. In

so far as situations are typical and recurrent in a given social structure, people develop names for them and strategies for handling them. Another name for strategies might be attitudes (PLF, p. 256).

Burke makes the same point again in saying that he thinks of poetry "as the adopting of various strategies for the encompassing of situations. These strategies size up the situations, name their structure and outstanding ingredients, and name them in a way that contains an attitude toward them" (PLF, p. 3). The phrase of interest here is "name their structure," for it reflects Burke's conviction that situations have structure which can be described equally well by a sociologist and a novelist or a poet. He thinks of the social structure, or the structure of any social situation, as the object of our understanding; and we can approach that social structure in a variety of ways, of which literature is one (that appeals to him very much). What he wants to do is to "take literature out of its separate bin and give it a place in a general 'sociological' picture" (PLF, p. 256).

2. Symbolic action.

One similarity between literature and sociological and psychological theory is that both involve words. Burke talks extensively about words as symbolic action and some attempt must be made to clarify his meaning. Attitudes embodied in literature and proverbs console us in certain situations; by symbolic action, Burke means that words—in proverbs, novels, or sociological theories—enable us to take attitudes towards things, enable us to take positions, and he sees the taking of a position as action. Thus, just as walking is an action in the usual straightforward sense, talking about walking would be, for Burke, symbolic action. The use of words in religious ritual is a clear-cut example of how words can involve symbolic action; the man says, "With this ring I thee wed," and those words constitute the act, they alter the world, they act on the world in a very obvious sense. Burke would maintain that any use of words involves acting on the world, even when the act is minimal, an act stripped down of its overt behavioral components and consisting entirely of the taking of an attitude, the espousal of a position vis-à-vis some aspect of reality. Obviously, both Laing and Goffman would agree; much of their work is an attempt to point out how each of us works on others by means of words and other acts. Words embody attitudes, and through our words we project our attitudes which in turn affect others and ourselves.

Of course, Burke admits freely that there is a difference between practical acts and symbolic acts:

> Still, there is a difference, and a radical difference, between building a house and writing a poem about building a house.... There are practical acts, and there are symbolic acts (nor should the distinction, clear enough in its extremes, be dropped simply because there is a borderline area wherein many practical acts take on a symbolic ingredient, as one may buy a certain commodity not merely to use it, but also because its possession testifies to his enrollment in a certain stratum of society) (PLF, p. 9).

For Burke, symbolic acts connect us with the world; through symbolic acts, we deal with the world, albeit not in exactly the same way as we deal with it in carrying out practical acts. More important, practical action depends on symbolic action:

> ... in a complex world, there are many kinds of action. Action requires programs—programs require vocabulary. To act wisely, in concert, we must use many words. If we use the wrong words, words that divide up the field inadequately, we obey false cues. We must name the friendly or unfriendly functions and relationships in such a way that we are able to do something about them (ATH, p. 4).[5]

5. ATH: *Attitudes Towards History*.

Thus, our symbolic action affects our practical action. Freud of course was fascinated by this phenomenon, as his way of accounting for hysterical paralysis makes clear. For Freud, a paralyzed arm was an expression—both symbolic and practical—of a hidden conflict. Freud diagnosed the symbolic component of the paralyzed arm.

Symbolic action can affect practical action, as shown by the following:

> All thought tends to name things not because they are precisely as named, but because they are not quite as named, and the name is designated as a somewhat hortatory device, to take up the slack. As others have pointed out, for instance, if the philosophy of "utilitarianism" were wholly correct, there would be no need for the philosophy. For men would spontaneously and inevitably follow the dictates of utility; whereas in actuality, the doctrine proclaiming the ubiquity of the utilitarian motive was formulated to serve as a plea for the deliberate consulting of the utilitarian motive (*A Grammar of Motives*, p. 54).

Here Burke makes a major point: ideas not only name or describe reality, but they encourage us to take a certain attitude toward that reality. This example is but one among many offered throughout his writing; he tries again and again to show how a theory, or any conceptual structure that purports to describe a real situation, implicitly argues for adopting a certain attitude toward it. Or, as he puts it elsewhere, most language has a suasive component (see his essay "Terministic Screens" in *Language as Symbolic Action*). Even what appears to be simple expository prose, as in a research report by a scientist, contains much persuasion. The scientist's persuasion is subtle, but nonetheless important. He is trying to persuade the reader of the legitimacy of his claim to the name "scientist" by his sober tone, by his careful diagrams and charts and tables, by his passive-voice prose, by the way he structures his article to conform with whatever standards exist in his particular field of science.

Moreover, he is trying to persuade the reader that his results are honestly and scrupulously arrived at, and that they are important.

In the same essay ("Terministic Screens") Burke extends this line of thought; in his words, "Even if a given terminology is a reflection of reality, by its very nature as a terminology it must be a selection of reality; and to this extent, it must function also as a deflection of reality" (LSA, p. 45).[6] In a sense, this is common knowledge. But the implications of this idea have not penetrated psychology. Connected with this observation is the notion that a terminology (theory with its concomitant vocabulary and conceptual structure) points a person in a particular direction: it helps him to see some things more easily, and inclines him to ignore other things. Burke offers three examples (from Watson and Bowlby, the psychologists, and from St. Augustine) and states:

> Our point is: all three terminologies directed the attention differently, and thus led to a correspondingly different quality of observations. In brief, "behavior" isn't something that you need but observe; even something so "objectively there" as behavior must be observed through one or another kind of terministic screen, that directs the attention in keeping with its nature (LSA, p. 49).

This is an extremely important point, considerably more subtle than—although intimately connected with—the point Rosenthal makes in his studies of experimental bias. The same point is often made in books on the philosophy of science (e.g., N. R. Hanson: *Patterns of Discovery*); observation is to some extent contingent on ideas (or on concepts, on theories, on vocabulary, etc.). The crucial phrase is the qualifier "to some extent"—obviously, people can to some extent (again) see around their concepts. As studies in

---

6. LSA: *Language as Symbolic Action.*

perceptual psychology have shown, people sometimes see what they want (expect) to see, but not always.

To return to Burke's statement: behavior is not simply "there" to be observed. This is the crux of what he says for us psychologists. We cannot simply observe behavior without having some idea (however faint and implicit; see Polanyi on the role of implicit ideas in scientific research) of what we are looking for. Burke would argue further that we always have a set of concepts which provide us with a way of categorizing what we see:

> We must use terministic screens, since we can't say anything without the use of terms; whatever terms we use, they necessarily constitute a corresponding kind of screen; and any such screen necessarily directs the attention to one field rather than another (LSA, p. 50).

It makes clear that observation prior to a theoretical understanding (however vague and unclear) of what is to be observed is not by any means a run-of-the-mill occurrence. This greatly qualifies one of the central tenets of the so-called scientific method—or what appears as such in the first chapters of many introductory psychology books—that science consists of observation which precedes theory-building.

Furthermore, Burke is saying—although it is not clear in this passage—that behavior involves motivation, and that our understanding of motivation is always an important factor in determining what we observe when we look at behavior. Behavior is not just there to be observed; although sheer motion and activity are there, such activity is a long way from behavior (see Chein's interesting book on this point, *The Science of Behavior and the Image of Man*).

3. Motivation and behavior.

Consider the following quotation from the introduction to Burke's book, *A Grammar of Motives:*

> What is involved, when we say what people are doing

and why they are doing it? An answer to that question
is the subject of this book. The book is concerned with
the basic forms of thought which, in accordance with
the nature of the world as all men necessarily experience it, are exemplified in the attributing of motives.
These forms of thought can be embodied profoundly
or trivially, truthfully or falsely. They are equally
present in systematically elaborated metaphysical
structures, in legal judgments, in poetry and fiction, in
political and scientific works, in news and in bits of
gossip offered at random (GM, p. x).[7]

The latter part of this passage repeats what we have already
reviewed: Burke's belief that literature and various kinds of
theory have something in common, insofar as each tries to
confront the world, to understand the structure of reality.
The beginning and middle parts of this quotation make
clear his interest in what are usually considered psychological questions: he talks of what people are doing and of
motivation, both clearly psychological topics.

Burke wants to study how we talk about what people do,
how we talk about why people do things; thus his work is
clearly closer in its emphasis on verbal structures to literary
criticism and philosophy than to psychology. But psychologists cannot evade many of the questions Burke raises
so acutely: how to define motivation, or what constitutes
behavior and what is the relation between overt action and
such internal action as taking an attitude.

Burke is concerned with understanding behavior and is
convinced of the necessity of looking beyond the overt
action component of behavior:

Two men, for instance, may be standing side by side
performing the same "operations," so far as the carrying out of instructions is concerned. Yet they are performing radically different acts if one is working for
charitable purposes and the other to the ends of ven-

7. GM: A Grammar of Motives.

geance. They are performing the same motions but different acts (GM, p. 108).

He finds it necessary to differentiate motion from act; he feels that motions get meaning from their context, and that the important context is often thoughts, or attitudes. The motion is the bare external sequence of movements; the act is constituted by the motion and the connections between the motion and the motive.

Burke's emphasis on connections shows the limitations of Freudian analysis of literature. Until now, Freud is the psychologist who has most influenced literary criticism; no other psychologist begins to approach the extent and depth of his influence. Freud's principal formula for the evaluation of literature is that of *wish-fulfillment*: he sees poems, novels, plays, as dreamlike; they represent the conflict between drives towards satisfaction of wishes on the one hand, and the controlling forces on the other. Burke's formula makes *communication* the important category for literary analysis:

> The primary category, for the explicit purposes of literary criticism, would thus seem to me to be that of communication rather than that of wish, with its disguises, frustrations, and fulfillments. Wishes themselves, in fact, become from this point of view analyzable as purposes that get their shape from the poet's perspective in general (while this perspective is in turn shaped by the collective medium of communication). The choice of communication also has the advantage, from the sociological point of view, that it resists the Freudian tendency to overplay the psychological factors. . . (PLF, p. 243).

A social psychologist might well agree with Burke that parts of Freudian theory do overemphasize the psychological in the sense of *seeming* to give great weight to purely internal individual motivations. But, in fact, Freud is more of a social psychologist—seeing individual motivations arising from a social context, primarily from a familial context—than he is ordinarily given credit for. Burke himself has pointed this out. In any case, the parts of Freudian theory used most imaginatively by literary critics are the individualistic psychodynamic parts, as Burke insists.

When Burke talks of communication, he means that art exists (and is effective in arousing and keeping people's interest) because the artist manages to talk about experiences in a way which communicates to people, which affects people. The experiences must be shared widely if the art is to communicate; given that the experiences are widely shared, the artist creates or discovers some symbolic structure—verbal or otherwise—which speaks to people or enables them to speak about the experience.[8] This approach leads Burke to be less concerned with whether a work of literature is good or bad, and more concerned with why it appeals (or does not appeal) to some specific group of people. He talks about how art communicates, and why.

4. People as actors-acters.

Verbal communication interests Burke most of all; and his view of words as forms of action, and his insistence that to understand words we must understand the context within which they are used, are both indicative of a social-psychological point of view. The following expresses both of these emphases:

> Words are aspects of a much wider communicative context, most of which is not verbal at all. Yet words also have a nature peculiarly their own. And when discussing them as modes of action, we must consider both this nature as words in themselves and the nature they get from the nonverbal scenes that support their acts (PLF, p. vii).

These emphases on words as action, and on context as important for meaning, are connected in his thinking with

8. See his essay "Lexicon Rhetoricae" in his book *Counter-Statement*.

his view of people as actors. He contrasts his view of people as actors with other prevalent views of people (as machines, as animals, as personalities); he confronts the heart of the psychological enterprise: how to define man.[9] His view of man as an actor is a traditional social-psychological view. Seeing man as an actor, using words to act on others and the world, is social-psychological in nature; it necessarily emphasizes the social context of the acts being performed. Burke explicitly talks of his theories as dramatic; they involve analysis of scenes, and of acts, as well as of actors. His view of man as an actor sets man squarely within society:

> People are neither animals nor machines (to be analyzed by the migration of metaphors from biology or mechanics), but actors and acters. They establish identity by relation to groups (with the result that, when tested by individualistic concepts of identity, they are felt to be moved by "deceptions" or "illusions," the irrational—for one's identification as a member of a group is a role, yet it is the only active mode of identification possible, as you will note, by observing how all individualistic concepts of identity dissolve into the nothingness of mysticism and the absolute). If you would avoid the antithesis of supernaturalism and naturalism, you must develop the coordinates of socialism—which gets us to cooperation, participation, man in society, man in drama (PLF, p. 268).

In this passage, Burke does not argue for the belief that man cannot be adequately defined as animal or machine, nor for his view that man is most properly viewed as actor and acter. There is not space here for a presentation of Burke's arguments on these issues, although they are interesting and would be worth comparing with similar arguments made by professional psychologists. For example, Isidor Chein is very

9. See his essay "Definition of Man" in *Language as Symbolic Action*, pp. 3-24.

concerned with just this issue: how do we psychologists define man implicitly by the way we treat him; and how should we define man to account for the data of man's existence.[10]

I want to draw attention to what has become a recurrent theme: the dissatisfaction expressed here with individualistic concepts of identity. Burke bears down on a central point here: if we are to acquire a social psychology, we need to work with different concepts, for the individualistic concepts of identity will not move us towards an adequate understanding of participation, of cooperation, of man in society.

EVALUATION

An oft-repeated criticism of Burke deserves some discussion, since it is accurate to some extent. Let us examine Sidney Hook's criticism, although there are other writers on Burke who make the same point (e.g., Louis Fraiberg, pp. 335-44, in Rueckert, *Critical Responses*).

> From the indisputable truth that a perspective enters into all thinking behavior, Burke goes to the highly dubious proposition that any perspective can be made to fit the deliverances of experience and vice versa. Nowhere is there adequate recognition of the objective compulsions of the realm of fact (Hook, p. 92, in Rueckert, *Critical Responses*).

This criticism of Burke is accurate insofar as it makes clear that Burke is in fact arguing that *any* perspective (theory, set of concepts, etc.) can be applied to the deliverances of experience. However, Hook is mistaken in assuming that Burke argues that any perspective can be made to fit since

10. See Isidor Chein: *The Science of Behavior and the Image of Man.* Further, most of the humanistic psychologists are concerned with this issue, with the way in which conventional psychology defines man as either machine, or animal, or object. These psychologists try to develop other definitions or conceptions of man (e.g., Abraham Maslow tries; as do Binswanger and the existential psychologists).

that word *fit* implies "with some exactness." Burke seems to argue not that all perspectives fit reality (experiences) equally well, but rather that the proponents of a particular point of view *make reality fit* their point of view. And Burke argues quite obviously that human beings have a fantastic capacity for cramming the facts of reality-experience into almost any conceivable theoretical conception. This is an important point; Hook's objection goes to the heart of what Burke is doing. Burke sometimes does seem to be saying what Hook says; but when all of his books are read, Burke quite clearly emerges as a man who is more concerned with how the human mind operates than with the truth or falsity of any one particular theory about reality.

More importantly, Burke assumes that there is some reality toward which each of us must have a point of view. And through his ceaseless efforts to show how one point of view (theory, position, perspective) can be translated into another (into any other, perhaps, depending on the translator), Burke seems to be placing a rather heavy emphasis on the way in which each person is somehow in touch with the same reality, the same world. It is the unremitting presence of this world which forces each of us to adopt some position toward it; and it is the fact that each of us—whether living in the second century B.C. or in the twentieth century A.D., whether male or female, whether living in the woods or in the city—is facing more or less the same real world, that makes the positions we each adopt towards it translatable, one into another.

To return to Hook's criticism of Burke: Hook states further that an error Burke is prone to is his "tendency to regard what is revealed in any one perspective of equal validity, in relation to a specific purpose, with what is revealed in any other" (p. 92). Hook omits the crucial fact that Burke is not so much interested in the validity of any one perspective as in the ways in which the sheer fact of the existence of so many different perspectives indicates something important about human beings. Hook is right in saying that Burke regards one perspective as being as useful to him as another. Useful for what? For making clear that the human is a perspective-generating animal. Burke is not primarily talking about the worth of the perspective—although he often seems to be; he is talking about the ways in which human beings generate these perspectives. Why do people generate so many different perspectives? That is the kind of question which interests Burke.

Many of Burke's ideas are not really new to psychology—for example, his discussion of motivation and behavior does not really add to analyses which have already been made by psychologists who are interested in philosophy and with conceptual clarification and definition (e.g., the work of Chein, or work published in the recent *Journal for the Theory of Social Behaviour*). But his concern with ideas coupled with a desire to understand people is valuable, expressed within a context which includes respect for not only psychological thought but philosophy and literature as well. As I said earlier, part of my aim is to persuade the reader that psychologists could benefit by more thoughtful contact with the thought of nonpsychologists, and thus in a sense Burke is merely an illustrative case for the purpose of this general argument.

But one theme in Burke's thought is of central substantive importance to this book: his analysis of words as symbolic acts and of symbolic action as an essential aspect of our behavior. This point is important since making symbolic action and communication central provides a way to see people as interconnected. His emphasis on symbolic action leads him to develop a concept of identity which underscores our connections with each other, rather than our separateness. By using words and through other symbolic actions, people take positions with regard to one another and the world. This notion is of course very similar to Goffman's idea that people might be defined as stance-taking entities, and stressing the position or stance one takes forces a recognition of the importance of the context within which the position is being taken.

Certain of Burke's intellectual proclivities make his writing and thinking pertinent to the social sciences and people concerned with social planning. Burke often attempts to stand things on their heads, to turn things upside-down intellectually, and this leads him in many different directions. For example, he shows that what we ordinarily consider vice—e.g., indolence—can come to seem a virtue. Indolence would be a virtue if it indicated the inability of a social system to inspire activity and involvement on the part of the individual. Thus, in observing a classroom where many children are working hard and some are not, we might say that only the latter are really worthwhile: only they can see the frivolity of the tasks demanded of them; only they have the inner nerve to refuse to do that which is asked of them. (Of course, this line of thought leads one to prefer a word other than *indolent* to describe the children.)

Burke's main thrust describes theories in general. He argues that any theory, by emphasizing certain aspects of reality, will de-emphasize and thus distort others insofar as it implies that the de-emphasized aspects are not very important at all. Burke's point is made concretely over and over again in his books; in discussing Freud, he makes clear that by directing our attention to certain categories of events (dreams, impulses, defenses against conflict) Freud takes our attention away from other things (the nature of the outer world the person lives in, what his job is like, his apartment, his neighbors). In another place, he points out that "Though the Freudian terminology . . . does lay major stress upon emancipating the patient, this very featuring of freedom deflects attention from the notably authoritarian aspects of psychotherapy, in the patient's subjection (however roundabout) to the analyst's role as priest of the confessional couch" (LSA, p. 80). The value of this kind of perspective on Freud's theory can be easily appreciated today when these small points made by Burke have been mined thoroughly for whatever of value lies in them by critics of Freudian theory and therapy. Burke's insights into the limitations of any theoretical viewpoint are part of his value for the social sciences.

Behind Burke's analysis of the distortions contained in any theoretical viewpoint lies a very complicated view of reality, part of which concerns the interpenetration of good and evil. Burke tries to show how anything good will have attendant bads; anything bad will have attendant goods. This position is enshrined for most of us in such platitudes as "It's an ill wind that blows nobody good," but even so, we have not really integrated this idea into our thinking. We are always looking for solutions to problems, and social scientists and planners in particular are often looked to as a group which can help find solutions (to problems of over-population, pollution, scarcity, war, racism, etc.). The problem, as we saw earlier with Skinner, is that social scientists and planners encourage this attitude on the part of others; they encourage being looked to for solutions. Yet it is conceivable, following Burke's line of thought, that solutions are improbable; one never entirely does away with bads. Every solution of a current problem may breed a new problem that will keep our lives hazardous. Our social planning, or public debate about social planning, could do with a healthy dose of this attitude as an antidote to the constant flurries of excitement over new solutions to particular problems.[11]

THOMAS SCHELLING

The writings of Thomas Schelling seem to embody a similar point of view. Schelling makes the kinds of points Burke seems to be making, but in a more accessible manner, and what Schelling has to say is important for any kind of social theory or planning. Schelling seems relatively unknown, compared to other social thinkers like Goffman, even though what he has to say is as striking and pertinent.[12]

11. Philip Slater, in his recent book, *Earthwalk* (New York: Doubleday, 1974), makes a similar argument much more thoroughly.

12. For some indication of how relatively unknown Schelling is within social psychology, consider that Roger Brown, in his useful and widely used text on social psychology, devotes a whole chapter to Schelling's specialty, but does not even mention Schelling, much less devote any space to reviewing his ideas. Deutsch and Krauss, in their *Theories in*

Schelling has published widely in the fields of economics, international relations, and social theory; we shall examine only those aspects of his thinking which are pertinent to general considerations of social theory. In particular, the discussion will focus on the two of his writings that deal with social theory: his book, *The Strategy of Conflict,* and his more recent article, "On the Ecology of Micromotives."

SCHELLING'S THOUGHT: GAME THEORY

Within social psychology, Schelling's position is often referred to as game theory. Game theory derives most obviously from von Neumann and Morgenstern's *Theory of Games and Economic Behavior;* it often takes a very quantitative form, as represented by Luce and Raiffa's *Games and Decisions;* but it need not, as Schelling makes clear. Behind game theory itself lies the belief that studying what people do while playing games helps us understand how people behave in some areas of everyday life; games offer a paradigm of some aspects of human behavior and simultaneously offer an opportunity for experimentation and some degree of rigor in quantitative model-building. Psychologists interested in game theory perform experiments in which two people (most typically only two) are asked to play some kind of game with each other according to certain rules and constraints; then the behavior of several dyads is observed; finally, some attempt is made to provide a model which would explain or describe what the various dyads did in the game they played. Game theorists try to take into account such factors as the possible moves that each player can make, the number of players, and the value to each player of each possible move or each possible outcome. In addition, the theorist needs to know whether the players trust each other, can communicate with one an-

Social Psychology devote eight pages to Goffman (and an entire chapter to role theory, which is the theoretical approach Goffman's name is connected with) but do not even mention Schelling. This, of course, does not mean that they were unfamiliar with Schelling's work.

other, and what they each expect of the other. It is these latter factors that Schelling finds most interesting.

1. Strategy.

Schelling is most interested in games involving strategy. In his words,

> the term 'strategy' is taken, here, from the theory of games, which distinguishes games of skill, games of chance, and games of strategy, the later being those in which the best course of action for each player depends on what the other players do. The term is intended to focus on the interdependence of the adversaries' decisions and on their expectations about each other's behavior (SC, p. 3).[13]

Schelling's interest in interdependence and expectations clearly makes this work part of social psychology.

People are interdependent in games of strategy insofar as what one person does affects what the other does; neither can act without taking into account both what the other just did and what he might do next. Chess is like this, of course; and just as some scientists are interested in designing a computer that will play chess, so some social psychologists are interested in designing highly mathematical models which would specify how people will react in games of a certain type. Just as chess seems susceptible to the rational logical analysis a machine could do quite well, referring to what people do with each other as games holds out the promise that once we grasp the structure of the game, we shall be able to predict how people playing the game will behave. We would be able to design computer simulations in which computers are programmed to behave as people would, so that for each small change in the rules of a given game, the computer would play out the possible outcomes in terms of changes in people's behavior.

However, Schelling's interest in games has led him in

---

13. SC: *Strategy of Conflict.*

another direction: he emphasizes the complexity of people's behavior, and points out how social situations are much more complex than most simple games (such as chess) and therefore not easily predictable. As he says:

> There is no way to build a model for the interaction of two or more decision units, with the behavior and expectations of those decision units being derived by purely formal deduction. An analyst can deduce the decisions of a single rational mind if he knows the criteria that govern the decisions; but he cannot infer by purely formal analysis what can pass between two centers of consciousness. It takes at least two people to test that. . . . Taking a hint is fundamentally different from deciphering a formal communication or solving a mathematical problem; it involves discovering a message that has been planted within a context by someone who thinks he shares with the recipient certain impressions or associations. One cannot, without empirical evidence, deduce what understandings can be perceived in a . . . game of maneuver any more than one can prove, by purely formal deduction, that a particular joke is bound to be funny (SC, pp. 163-64).

Given Schelling's fidelity to the complexity of everyday life situations (e.g., taking a hint), his interest in game theory is less in quantitative model-building than in the way games can be used to provide concrete illustrations of capacities people have which are used in everyday life but which are not clearly visible ordinarily, since they occur in a context where they are difficult to perceive.

2. Tacit coordination and convergent expectations.

One of Schelling's games illustrates peoples' capacity for what he calls tacit coordination (where no communication is possible). He tells a group of people that they are each to guess a number simultaneously between 1 and 10, each one trying to guess the same number. If all guess the same number, they win a prize. They are not allowed to talk or communicate in any way. Schelling reports that two-fifths of the people he asked to do this guessed the number 1. In a similar game, each of two people is asked to divide a pile of $100 into two parts. Each is supposed to try to divide the pile the same way; if they do, they get a prize. In this example, 36 out of 41 people divided the pile into two $50 piles. Schelling's examples continue (see *Strategy of Conflict*, pp. 54-58) but his general point is that

> People can often concert their intentions or expectations with others if each knows that the other is trying to do the same. Most situations—perhaps every situation for people who are practiced at this kind of game—provide some clue for coordinating behavior, some focal point for each person's expectation of what the other expects him to expect to be expected to do (SC, p. 57).

Schelling calls this tacit coordination and believes it is a general feature of everyday social life.

How does knowing this help us understand larger social realities? Here Schelling makes his real contribution; he shows us how to gain a better understanding of such phenomena as pollution and housing segregation, using the basic understanding of people which is apparent in such simple games. Let us first briefly review some of the other concepts he uses to analyze games, and then show how he uses these concepts to help us understand some—but not all—general social problems.

Basic to Schelling's notion of tacit coordination is the idea of convergent expectations. Different people may have expectations which converge on some focal point, as in the examples just given; a feature of social life is that convergent expectations create some social realities that would change if the expectations did. In a sense, this is a social version of the self-fulfilling prophecy. Schelling's interest in coordination extends to situations where communication is possible; then what occurs may be simple (two people walking down a street in opposite directions avoid bumping into each other; they are coordinating in a simple fashion), or complex, in which case bargaining often occurs.

When a house is being sold, the buyer and seller have complementing interests, to some extent, but they also have competing interests; therefore they bargain. Schelling is interested in the psychological aspects of bargaining, and in the way that the same factors (intuitive and tacit) that were involved in tacit coordination are often involved even where bargaining is explicit. Often there is the same reliance on some focal point which may seem as arbitrary as that fixed on where communication is not possible. Schelling offers as one example "the speed with which a number of Middle Eastern oil-royalty arrangements converged on the 50-50 formula a few years after World War II" (SC, footnote, p. 68). Similarly, when a house is being sold, the buyer and seller are often involved in a process involving some degree of intuitively perceived mutual expectations: a lot of the bargaining remains implicit even in a situation where some of it is explicit.

3. Commitment.

Schelling devotes some attention to *commitment* as a factor in bargaining and coordination. Commitment is the psychological process of fixing on some course of action. It plays a role in bargaining when one makes his commitment clear to the other. A person selling a house may be committed to a rock-bottom price of $30,000. If he can make this clear to the buyers, then he has a good chance of getting the $30,000 if the buyers really want the house. The problems arise in communicating the truth of the situation: how does one make his expectations clear to the other?

In driving, one can shut oneself off from communication and step on the accelerator; one acts as though one is going to be allowed to get into the lane of traffic, and by looking straight ahead, one cuts himself off from further communication on the matter. Other drivers are a problem; one must simultaneously communicate his intention (commitment) and shut himself off from arguing about it. This is not so easy, of course; but this is the kind of social situation Schelling is interested in analyzing.

4. Coordination, conflict, and bargaining.

Most generally, Schelling's interests are in coordination and conflict, and in situations where some elements of both exist. He always uses analyses of games as a way of illuminating larger social situations; but whereas his main interest in his 1960 book *(Strategy of Conflict)* was international relations, the 1971 article ("On the Ecology of Micromotives") is oriented more toward domestic problems: pollution, segregated housing, etc. This article shows how certain social situations (resulting from the aggregate actions of many individual people) can emerge from a variety of different kinds of individual motivational patterns, and there is no way to be certain what individual motivations led to a given general outcome. For example, given that a dirty environment exists, we cannot know for certain what individual motivations lead to this general result. Given that segregated housing exists, we cannot know for certain what individual motivations combine to produce the general result.

To link Schelling's argument here with his earlier book; because social life constitutes a situation in which bargaining must occur where not all the relevant parties are available for participation, where communication is not always possible for a variety of reasons, then inevitably results are generated which no one in particular wants but which everyone feels powerless to avoid (e.g. overcrowded highways).

SCHELLING'S ANALYSIS OF SOME SOCIAL PROBLEMS

Let us examine some of Schelling's examples. The kind of bargaining which involves parties who cannot be present is illustrated by pollution. Pollution exists today in some parts of our country partly because years ago people did not worry about the long-range effects of certain behavior. The people alive today constitute a relevant party in the social situation of 1900, but the people alive today did not participate in the decision-making that occurred in 1900; so the people in 1900 could easily ignore the desires and wishes of the people of 1970. Similarly, today part of our concern with pollution arises because we are essentially giving a voice to unborn generations who are yet to come.

Similarly, people from one country kill ocean fish without first consulting people from other countries. Once there was no ready mechanism enabling people from different countries to negotiate with one another about deep-sea fishing rights. Similarly, there is often no ready mechanism enabling residents of a neighborhood to negotiate with one another about noise pollution on Sunday morning. No one wants lawn-mower noise, perhaps, but no one knows for certain that everyone else will refrain from mowing; all the parties concerned cannot meet around a conference table because there is no viable social mechanism enabling them to do so. Thus Schelling sees a bargaining situation where the bargaining cannot occur explicitly; then it often goes on implicitly, to the detriment of everyone's interests.

Traffic problems provide abundant examples of what Schelling is talking about, since presumably no one wants traffic jams. Yet traffic jams occur, according to Schelling, because people do not have a mechanism enabling them to bargain with one another for a viable method of coping with the problem. Thus Schelling sees people not as evil (intending harm to others), not as stupid (unable to see the effects of their actions), but rather as helpless because they lack effective social mechanisms for explicit bargaining.

Schelling tries to relate present-day social problems to his analyses of game situations in his earlier book in discussing the way in which each person's actions affect others, even though the person has no way of accurately predicting what the effects on others will be. For example, when a person moves from one house to another, both neighborhoods change. The difference is small, but not negligible, as Schelling demonstrates in a game he invents involving the use of dimes and pennies (or any two different kinds of markers) on a gridlike board similar to a checkerboard.

Schelling illustrates how segregated neighborhoods may occur even when no one wants them. He sets up a game where he assumes that neither dimes nor pennies want to live in entirely segregated neighborhoods, but both dimes and pennies want some of their close neighbors to be similar to themselves. The assumptions used in playing the game may vary; but the game involves making some assumption (both dimes and pennies want at least half of their close neighbors to be similar to themselves), choosing some number of dimes and pennies so that the total number will not fill up whatever size grid you are playing on, and then arranging the dimes and pennies on the board so that each is happy (according to the simple assumption about the kinds of neighbors each wants). Then move one of the dimes or pennies to an empty square. See whether this changes either the old or the new neighborhood enough to make some of the residents unhappy. Depending on the rules, the numbers of empty squares, and the proportions of dimes and pennies used, the housing situation will be more or less precariously balanced. Some situations will have more free-dom of movement than others. In some situations, one or two people (coins) moving will upset the whole situation; in others as many as 10 percent of the people can move without the situation becoming upset.

Schelling's main argument remains: there is no social mechanism or arrangement set up whereby people can articulate their desires and then negotiate with one another so as to satisfy them most effectively. Instead, there is a bargaining situation with no communication. The result can often be many people living in segregated neighborhoods even though they prefer to live in mixed neighborhoods which would not become unbalanced heavily in favor of the other kind of people. Schelling's point is not to argue about what people really want, but rather to show that assuming certain wants, a social situation can arise in which those wants are guaranteed not to be satisfied. And this can occur, according to his model, without any malevolence on anyone's part.

Schelling is naturally interested in effective social regulating mechanisms. His favorite example seems to be the traffic light, which sets up a self-enforcing system which (so long as it is working adequately) guarantees everyone a turn. And in some situations, this is the most that people can reasonably hope for. Given a scarcity of the good, whatever it may be—in this situation, it is available road space for one's vehicle—the good must be rationed and people given turns.

Schelling thinks that our present social situation is characterized (certainly with pollution) by an abundance of bads, rather than by a scarcity of goods. Although pollution still exists, he seems to think that, in principle, the ways to cope with it are already available, but call for new principles of organization. His suggestions in this respect are not so interesting as his forceful argument that in many respects we are in a no-win situation: there is no one strategy which will produce a victory over the problems that beset us. Rather he thinks that every strategy has its costs. In his words, "We have to pay a price for victory, and we usually have to pay it in the same currency in which we enjoy it. A good many bads are merely the reverse side of some goods; and the ratio of bad to good depends on the particular uses and beneficiaries and victims.... Under this no-win philosophy the object is to discriminate against the goods that entail a disproportionate volume of bads..." ("On the Ecology of Micromotives," p. 95). This is the point at which our analysis of Schelling's ideas began, as we compared Schelling's insistence on the way in which bad things come entangled with good things to Kenneth Burke's similar insistence.

One of Schelling's vivid illustrations concerns penicillin, which reduces or even eliminates certain kinds of bads (risks associated with some diseases). Yet, as we know so well now, the more we use penicillin (or any similar agent for eliminating some pest or germ: e.g., DDT), the more we contribute to the rise of penicillin-resistant bacteria. Hans Zinsser puts it well in his fascinating history of typhus: "It is not at all unlikely that the successful control of an epidemic disease through several generations may interfere with the more permanently effective, though far more cruel, processes by which nature gradually immunizes a race" (pp. 50-51). This is another situation in which future generations ought to have a voice and yet do not; we may be reducing our own illnesses at the price of increasing theirs later. It is hard to tell what the long-term bad results of present-day goods may be, but—in Schelling's view—we are virtually guaranteed some bad results. One of the major empirical problems is that often the ratio of good to bad alters so slowly and over such a long time span that we have no easy way of calculating it.

EVALUATION

Schelling's major points in his article are (a) Aggregate phenomena such as traffic or pollution patterns in a city are not linked in any obvious way to individual motivational decisions; one cannot determine individuals' wants by examining large social patterns. Thus, segregated housing does not necessarily mean that some people like things that way. Traffic jams do not necessarily mean that people like traffic jams. (b) Bad things and good things come intermingled; hoping to eliminate a bad completely is always illusory.

Schelling's major contribution to the discussion of such social problems as pollution and segregation is his idea that we have something to gain from considering the structural determinants of these problems. Just as the structure of certain games (e.g. Prisoner's Dilemma) virtually guarantees that both participants will end up unhappy, so the structure of some social situations virtually guarantees that no one will end up happy.[4] This interpretation offers grounds for

4. The Prisoner's Dilemma arises as follows. Two men are arrested and charged with committing a crime. The police have enough evidence to be sure the men did the crime, but not enough to get them convicted. Each

optimism to those who are looking for such grounds, insofar as it implies that our present-day problems are not due to irreducible human evil or stupidity, but rather to faulty social arrangements.

Criticism of our faulty social structure has become routine in the past five or ten years, but Schelling offers a different rationale for criticizing it. He does not assume a power elite ruling things for its own benefit; he does not assume class rivalry or economic determinants of social problems. He uses game theory and his earlier speculations about human problems involving coordination and conflict as ways of looking at our present social situation.

Schelling's analysis obviously slights the psychological realm; he elides the difficult problem of assessing needs and motives by hypothesizing certain motives, and then showing what kinds of large-scale social results are likely given the hypothetical motives. Furthermore, there are many structural determinants of social situations which he ignores, e.g., that some people's motives are more influential than others. Depending on your social position, you will be more or less influential than someone else in determining the aggregate social result.

But although his analyses are far from complete, Schelling makes a signal contribution to our discussions by giving one indication of how to move beyond the kinds of simple analyses of social situations which have at their root an image of two people (or factions or classes) fighting with one another, in which the stronger side inevitably wins. Schelling gives numerous illustrations of the greater com-

---

man is therefore offered a deal: if he confesses and the other man does not, his sentence will be very light. For example, if A confesses and B does not, A will get six months or so in prison, while B will get 20 years. But if both confess, each will get 8 years. If neither confesses, they will have to be charged with some other (minor) crime and they will each get 2 years or so. They are in separate cells, and so cannot talk; but if they trust each other, neither will confess. But they cannot communicate, and so do not know what the other is thinking. That creates the dilemma. The structure of the situation leads each to hope to get the minimum sentence (six months); and thus each will get 8 years.

plexity needed to analyze social situations and do justice to them. Conflict in itself is a complicated category, and in order to understand conflict we must know many parameters of the conflict situation. Is communication permitted, or does the sheer structure of the situation minimize the possibility of communication and therefore to some degree shape the pattern of the conflict.

Schelling states that underlying our very human capacity for conflict is an equal capacity for coordination. Both conflict and coordination involve some mutual orientation: his concept of *convergent expectations* pertains to that kind of mutual orientation.

CHAPTER 8

Overview

Having reviewed ideas of several social theorists, what can we say now about various criticisms of the destructive effects of social institutions upon human functioning and experience? If psychology is to be of genuine service, it must confront those social criticisms. My belief is that psychology does have insight into certain aspects of the complex interconnections between man and society, and that it is ample for such a confrontation. That insight derives from the theoretical approaches we have discussed. Because theory is not given high value in social psychology, the importance of these theoretical positions is underestimated. Therefore our aim has not been simply to acquaint the reader with these theoretical approaches, to indicate how they illuminate some social criticism, and to show how each, taken on its own grounds, has conceptual problems; but also to persuade the reader that there is some purpose in a sustained analysis of such theoretical positions. There is value in trying to connect them, in trying to peer into their hidden assumptions, in trying to figure out the systematic theory which often underlies the surface presentation of ideas by these various writers.

My overriding concern is what I call the conceptual poverty of psychology, which is unlikely to be markedly reduced by a continued overestimation of the value of empirical research. Theory must be viewed as important if social

201

psychology is to prosper, and we psychologists must take more seriously the task of connecting our theoretical power with the social scene around us, rather than letting our practical efforts lie simply in our doing *ad hoc* analyses of social problems as they arise (welfare, war, day care, poverty, racism, etc.).

The main conclusion to be drawn from the arguments examined in this book has three parts. First, much social criticism seems inspired by the conception of an individual as one who is or should become truly autonomous and radically free of social constraint. Second, this social criticism sees the society which constrains the individual as relatively unitary in its oppressive power. Third, this social criticism, which conceives of an autonomous and unitary individual who is being damaged by an oppressive external unified society, is inadequate to what we know of both people and society. People and society might better be conceived of as complicated, made up of numerous parts intertwined with one another in ways which are complicated beyond the powers of simple description.

Let us examine the notion of the autonomous self. We have seen the connection between the ideas of Marcuse and Laing on the one hand, and social criticism on the other. Both Laing and Marcuse idealize a society which would permit the free flowering of individual autonomous selves. Marcuse argues that our present one-dimensional society has eradicated (or thoroughly undermined) the possibility of any conflict between the free self, on the one hand, and the society on the other. Marcuse pictures society as oppressive, damaging the individual people who live in it. Laing shows us a divided self which cannot find harmony and satisfaction because of the inroads made by a damaging social reality. The underlying ideal animating this criticism is of a unified self, free of the constraints of sociability. This thought underlies much contemporary social criticism which usually paints in rather broad strokes a portrait of a society crushing individual selves.

But does this picture make any sense? I have argued that Marcuse and Laing both undercut the validity of this picture by their persuasive arguments that people cannot possibly be free of society and its pressures, that people are inevitably bound up with society, that they influence one another constantly, that they are complicated even within themselves, and that any simple opposition of people on the one hand and society on the other is greatly misleading.

I have drawn attention to those parts of Laing's argument that show both (a) how the child is influenced subtly by his parents and his surrounding social context; and (b) how each of us, once grown, influences and is influenced by others. This picture of the relation between people and society fits in with much of what not only social psychology but also developmental and clinical psychology tell us.

Part of my attempt has been to show how the simple picture of people vs. society which underlies much contemporary social criticism, which animates much (but far from all) of the analysis given by both Laing and Marcuse, is also present in the relatively recent Third Force or humanistic psychology as represented by Carl Rogers, and, even more crucially, that it arises out of rather deep roots in American culture. Americans have long been accustomed to thinking in these simple terms: the individual is opposed to society; the rights of the individual are on the one hand, and the rights of society are on the other; people must endeavor to shake free of the clutches of society, must be wary of forces toward conformity, must not give in to social pressures. I briefly discussed several acute analyses of this strain in American culture contained in the writings of such literary critics as Quentin Anderson and Richard Poirier.

Anderson shows us the tendencies toward what he calls an imperial self, free from all social constraint. Poirier talks of the attempt, revealed in much of American literature, to "appropriate space to one's own desires," which I feel is a large component of the present popularity of both encounter groups and the humanistic psychology movement in general.

Carl Rogers may not talk of appropriating space to one's own desires, but he certainly talks of how each of us must find our own true self, must be what we are, must not give in to social pressures, but do what suits us as individuals rather than what suits the society around us. Although this is not his only theme—for he also talks of concern for others—the category of the "other" remains rather shadowy in his writings, and this is no accident. Inevitably Rogers considers the "other" in writing about marriage, about encounter groups, and about therapy; but his focus is always on the individual self, whose main concern ought to be to his own true desires. This erection of one's own true desires as a standard for the conduct of life is perhaps peculiarly American. In any case, there is little question that this standard is inadequate as a portrait of what people are like. To put it quite simply, people do not have their own desires in any simple sense. Their desires are shot through with social components at every level but the biological,[1] and although one can talk of true individuality at that level (in the quality and quantity, perhaps, of biological drives), and although the Freudian picture of people arises from just such a biological conception of individual drives in opposition to society, Rogers is obviously not concerned with the biological level.

In this light, let us consider the criticism of Rogers offered by Viktor Frankl in his article, "Beyond Self-Actualization and Self-Expression." Frankl is a psychologist who represents the European humanistic psychology movement. Although Frankl and other existential psychologists (Binswanger, Boss, et al.) are often grouped together with such humanists as Rogers and Maslow, they do have a few real differences of opinion. One such difference is reflected in the following, in which Frankl is discussing his form of therapy which he calls *logotherapy*:

According to logotherapeutic concepts, man is not primarily interested in any psychic conditions of his own, but rather is oriented toward the world, toward

1. And even here, what we conceive of as biological (e.g., sexuality) is permeated by sociality, as John Gagnon argues very acutely. See John Gagnon, "The Creation of the Sexual in Early Adolescence," in Jerome Kagan and Robert Coles, eds., *12-16: Early Adolescence* (New York: Norton, 1972), pp. 231-57.

the world of potential meanings and values which so-
to-speak are waiting to be fulfilled and actualized by
him. (p.7)

Frankl's reaction in contrasting an orientation towards psychic conditions of one's own, on the one hand, and the
world of potential meanings on the other, is in part what we
have been discussing in Rogers, who often seems to be
arguing that people should be primarily oriented toward
their own psychic states, toward becoming happy, becoming
contented, becoming free from pain and blocked feeling.
The result of this emphasis is a devaluation of the other, of
both the world in general outside of one and of other
people. In Frankl's words, again:

> ... the main mistake consists in the fact that appoint-
> ing self-realization as "the ultimate motive" would ...
> devaluate the world and its objects to mere means to
> an end. As a matter of fact, A. H. Maslow explicitly
> contends that "the environment is no more than
> means to the person's self-actualizing ends." So now
> we must pose the crucial question whether or not
> man's primary intention, or even his ultimate destina-
> tion could ever be properly circumscribed by the term
> "self-actualization." I would venture a strictly negative
> response to this question. It appears to me to be quite
> obvious that self-actualization is an effect and cannot
> be the object of intention (pp. 12-13).

Here Frankl's quote from Maslow ("the environment is no
more than the means to the person's self-actualizing ends")
can be seen as fitting together very neatly with Poirier's
analysis *(A World Elsewhere)* of those tendencies in American literature toward appropriating space to one's own
desires.[2]

---

2. The connection with our environmental crisis is perhaps also all too
clear, and if I understand Philip Slater correctly this is part of the
argument he makes in *Earthwalk* (New York: Doubleday, 1974).

As Poirier puts it:

> ... American literature does offer the most persistent, the most poignantly heroic examples of a recurrent literary compulsion, not at all confined to our literature, to believe in the possibilities of a new style. The new American style was meant to release hitherto unexpressed dimensions of the self into space where it would encounter none of the antagonistic social systems which stifle it in the more enclosed and cultivated spaces of England... (pp. 39-40).

Poirier seems to be talking of the same self that Rogers is discussing, a self which strives to make its own world for itself, in a space unencumbered by society and its fabrications (Poirier, p. 30). Just as Rogers contrasts the real self with the social self, so does a similar contrast run through much of American literature:

> ... Salinger's Holden Caulfield is a merely stock character enacting the American hero's effort, more significantly illustrated by Isabel Archer, to express the natural self rather than merely to represent, in speech and manner, some preordained social type (Poirier, p. 27).

This contrast between the natural self and the social self, or between the real self and the facade is basic not only to American literature in Poirier's diagnosis; not only to humanistic psychology, as represented by Rogers; but also to the social criticism of both Laing and Marcuse, and of other writers as well. This contrast not only animates much of our contemporary social criticism, but also seems basic to a typically American way of thinking about how people are related to culture. Jules Henry, the anthropologist, makes a very similar distinction between the inner self and the social facade:

How does society make people excruciatingly sensitive

to the possibilities of and dangers in losing reputation and how does society make one sensitive to one's vulnerability? It is done through placing reputation—the social person—in the centre of consideration and making reputation destiny; by degrading the *inner* self to second, third, or merely adventituous place, and making the social facade supreme, so that at every step the self will be sacrificed to the facade (in the essay "Vulnerability," in *On Sham and Vulnerability*, p. 88).

Here again is the contrast between the inner self and the social facade, the same contrast that we have seen Carl Rogers making. It is perhaps worth noting that Henry's analysis of sham gets into the same difficulties as Laing's analysis of the divided self: just as Laing says that schizophrenia is characterized by a divided self, goes on to recognize that everyone is divided, and concludes in part that we are all schizophrenic, so Henry argues that sham (pretending, trying to maintain an appearance which is discrepant from reality) is at the basis of schizophrenia, recognizes that there is a lot of sham throughout society, and concludes by anticipating a geometric increase in madness (Henry, *On Sham and Vulnerability*, p. 124).

A more fruitful way of analyzing the relations between self and society would be to follow up points which are hinted at in Laing and Marcuse, and which are made more explicitly in Goffman, and argue that any person is inevitably divided, and that this division is a product of the way he is born (weak and helpless) combined with the way he is raised (in a world filled with more powerful adults who affect him constantly), compounded by the fact that society is divided into parts each of which affects the child both by forming him or her, and by providing the growing person with something to react against. Ernest Becker, in an exciting attempt to integrate psychological thought with sociological and anthropological thinking (*The Birth and Death of Meaning*) puts it this way:

If man is the only animal whose consciousness of self gives him an unusual dignity in the animal kingdom, he also pays a tragic price for it. The fact that the child has to identify *first* means that his very first identity is a social product. His habitation of his own body is built from the outside in, not from the inside out. He doesn't unfold into the world, the world unfolds into him. As the child responds to the vocal symbols learned from his object, he often gives the pathetic impression of being a true social puppet, jerked by alien symbols and sounds. What sensitive parent does not have his satisfaction tinged with sadness as the child repeats with such vital earnestness the little symbols that are taught him? (p. 25)

The crucial sentence is "His habitation of his own body is built from the outside in, not from the inside out." The point is that same one made earlier in the chapters discussing Marcuse, Laing, and Goffman. People *become* in a social context; people grow up in a social situation and are irretrievably social themselves to some degree.

Sociologists have argued this point for a long time. For example, Peter Berger (in *Invitation to Sociology*) argues:

Meaning systems are socially constructed. The Chinese "brainwasher" conspires with his victim in fabricating a new life-story for the latter, just as does the psychoanalyst with his patient. Of course, in both situations the victim-patient comes to believe that he is "discovering" truths about himself that were there long before this particular conspiracy got under way. The sociologist will be, at the very least, skeptical about his conviction. He will strongly suspect that what appears as discovery is really invention. And he will know that the plausibility of what is thus invented is in direct relation to the strength of the social situation within which the invention is concocted (pp. 64-65).

Or, as he puts it more succinctly, ". . . even identities that we consider to be our essential selves have been socially assigned" (p. 98). Thus the conventional sociological view, as presented by Berger, is that identity and self are socially constituted. And Laing's books offer a powerful psychological perspective on how this happens with children in families, and how it continues in dyadic interactions.

The problem with this point of view is that it seems to offer too little scope for individual independence of social forces. Although Berger says that the genius and the madman escape this kind of sweeping social influence (p. 64), we have a sense that others of us as well escape to some degree. Here are two views of how that escape occurs.

One view is implicit in our analysis of the role that Freud's thinking plays in the social criticism of Laing and Marcuse. Freud's thought cuts in two opposing directions. On the one hand, his thought shows how we are each implicated in culture, as Lionel Trilling has it:

> It was he [Freud] who made it apparent to us how entirely implicated in culture we all are. By what he said or suggested of the depth and subtlety of the influence of the family upon the individual, he made plain how the culture suffuses the remotest parts of the individual mind, being taken in almost literally with the mother's milk. His psychology involves culture in its very essence—it tells us that the surrogates of culture are established in the mind itself, that the development of the individual mind recapitulates the development of culture (Essay, "Freud: Within and Beyond Culture," in *Beyond Culture*, p. 105).

But as Trilling also points out, there is an opposing edge to Freud's thought, which is at root biological, which leads Freud to postulate an unavoidable opposition between people and society:

> . . . I think we must stop to consider whether this emphasis on biology . . . is not so far from being a reac-

tionary idea that it is actually a liberating idea. It proposes to us that culture is not all powerful. It suggests that there is a residue of human quality beyond the reach of cultural control, and that this residue of human quality, elemental as it may be, serves to bring culture itself under criticism and keeps it from being absolute (p. 113).

Thus Freud postulates biological needs in each of us which are frustrated by any society; thus he (unwittingly perhaps) provided ammunition for the contemporary radical critiques of our society. Freud helped us see how individual people at least to some degree stand inevitably opposed to society and culture.

However there is another argument, which I make explicit, which helps us see how people escape total domination by any society. The argument hinges on the view of both individual and society as divided, made up of many parts, as shown in discussing Laing and Goffman. Each person is divided, composed of different parts. These parts may or may not be multiple at birth; there may be many needs within each of us at birth which, insofar as they are not unified, provide separate kinds of pressures within each of us, pushing us first in one direction, then in another. But the more significant development of inner division comes as children grow up in a social context. Then each child is confronted first with physical reality, which opposes him or her in various ways; second, with multiple sources of social pressure: from each of the adults who surround him, those he knows personally and those he knows indirectly through television, and later, from the magazines and books he reads. Thus one key to understanding how the individual is divided is seeing that society is divided. So long as society is made up of different parts, each exerting pressure in its own way on each person, then each person will develop different ways of dealing with each of those segments of society. As Goffman said, we each have conflicting dedications and, in a sense, those are our strength; whenever any one segment of society is putting too much pressure on us, there are other parts to turn to for support and help.

At this point we should remind ourselves of the concept of a good society which is implicit in contemporary social criticism and in the writings of Laing and Marcuse. The good society is discussed as though it forms an integrated harmonious whole. Such a discussion of the good society is harmful, if my present analysis is correct. My contention is that even though a society made up of many opposing parts creates conflict, 'that conflict is vital to the processes of change; this is true on an individual level as well as on the societal level. Just as change arises from conflict in society, so change arises from conflict in the individual. The great advantage of making the conception of division basic to our views both of individuals and societies is that it gives us a lever for explaining how change occurs. Within each individual, different segments of one's personality argue with one another, each of them tugging in a different direction. Each listens to different voices from the outside; each is susceptible to different kinds of pressures. Similarly, within society, different segments of the social structure argue with one another, and from this conflictual process may come change.

This is not to say that all division is beneficial, that conflict is inevitably good and therefore to be desired. At a very simple level of analysis, we can see that some kinds of conflict are more harmful than others; any conflict where one side is vastly more powerful than the other is not the kind of conflict that is going to lead to any change other than the oppression or elimination of the minority group. Neither is my point to glorify the pluralistic society in the way that American politicians often do. What is called the pluralistic society is all too often something else, as many of our best social critics have made clear; an apparent pluralism covers a situation where one group may have vastly more power than another. Finally, conflict and division within either the individual or society do not, obviously, always lead to change; nor if change does occur, is there any guarantee that it will be beneficial. On the level of the individual person, division may sometimes lead to nothing but painful stalemate, with no change occurring; but this only indicates that division is not the sole condition of change, nor any guarantor of beneficial change.

There are other advantages to a model of the individual and of society which enforce a conception of division rather than of harmony. Staying at the level of the individual and dyadic relations for a moment, we can argue that if each of us were truly a unified whole, we would find understanding a different other, or cooperating with a different other, very difficult. Bettelheim makes this point in discussing character development on the Israeli kibbutz. He is discussing the way in which people cope with losses of others (or fear of losing the other) by introjecting the other.

Laing discusses introjection and similar psychological processes, in which each of us psychologically takes parts of others inside us. Another writer makes the same point in the following:

> We do not know exactly how these universal mechanisms work but we see the end result in both clinical and everyday experience: each of us is in some ways a grotesque collage, a composite of injected and ejected parts over which we have no honest control. We are not aware that we carry such a burden of foreign matter in our amoebic pseudopods, nor do we know where the heart of our self really is, or clearly what images and things compose it (Ernest Becker, pp. 35-36).

Of course, part of Laing's point was that this burden of introjects undoes us; we become divided and lose our coherence. I submit that these introjects are no burden; in the following passage, Bettelheim suggests that having these introjects makes us more capable of understanding different other people:

> ... in a strange way these introjects are what later endow the child in our culture with both a deep em-

pathy for others (because he carries some other person within him), and a capacity for living independently (because with introjects to keep him company, independence is never again a being wholly alone) (Bettelheim, p. 189).

And speaking of the kibbutz child, Bettelheim argues that "... these youngsters have not introjected persons with whom they hold inner conversations, talks that require them to recognize the introject's viewpoint and their own at the same time" (p. 191).

Bettelheim makes two arguments in favor of introjection: it facilitates having conversations with others of different points of view; we can more easily (if not fully) understand that there are people with viewpoints different from our own, given that we have bits and pieces ("we are grotesque collages") of others within us. Second, Bettelheim argues that having this internal complexity, we are more easily able to be independent, both to oppose pressures from others and to live alone. With internal complexity, we are never completely alone (we have internal dialogues to occupy us); and with the internal diversity, we are better able to resist pressures from any one outside point. Bettelheim does not make this last point explicitly; but it flows from his analysis, and it of course is a basic part of the analysis we present here. If we have multiple internal parts, when any pressure arises from one segment of outside society, we can resist that pressure because we have within us the capacity to resist it; within us, we have parts which are more responsive to other segments of the outside world, and we gain footing for resisting one form of social pressure by allying ourselves with other segments of society. A young man about to be drafted can gain support for resisting the draft from reading Thoreau, or from talking with selected other people. He may be punished for his draft resistance, punished by "society," but in reality he is being punished and rewarded for the same act by different components of society.

Thus when we examine, as Bettelheim did, the ways in which children are raised in our society, and look for the influences of society, what we find are numerous influences from many segments of society, each working in slightly different directions. And if we try, as do Laing and Marcuse, in part, as do many social critics *in toto,* to find that society's influence is totally a corrupting one, we get into difficulty, for the indications are that a baby cannot become a person without some kind of help from others, and although that help is always "tainted" with definitions of reality, with assumptions about the nature of social forms, it also has a developing function. We tend today too much to oppose the corrupting and developing functions as though they were mutually exclusive. In remembering John Holt's distinction between molding a child and letting it grow, let us take that contrast as emblematic of that between corrupting and developing a child; we can see that the tendency is all too often to take that contrast as though it represents two mutually exclusive opposites.

In his biography of Matthew Arnold, Trilling also seems to oppose development and corruption:

> If the Victorian too much disregarded Rousseau and Wordsworth and thought of children as adults manquées, we today are perhaps too often tempted to think of adults as children manquées.... If for Wordsworth the influence of society was bound to corrupt the child, for Arnold it was likely to develop him; and his view is the more usable as it is the more logical of the two, if one admits that society has the means to develop without corrupting. (pp. 63-64)

But my analysis has pointed to the way in which these two are always intermingled. Children cannot be developed without being corrupted, if one chooses to use these terms. Or, if you will, children cannot be corrupted without being simultaneously developed.

Gordon Allport reaches the same point in a succinct statement:

> Thus there seem to be two contrary forces at work.

The one makes for a closed tribal being. It takes its start in the dependence of the child upon those who care for him. His gratifications and his security come from the outside; so too do all the first lessons he learns; the times of day when he may have meals, the activities for which he is punished and those that bring reward. He is coerced and cajoled into conformity but not, we note, with complete success. He shows a capacity even from birth to resist the impact of maternal and tribal demands. While to a certain degree his group shapes his course, at the same time it seems to antagonize him, as if he realized its threat to his integrity (Allport, p. 35).

This is one of the central points, which I have now made in a variety of ways. I have argued that people are complicated, that society is complicated, that people develop in and through society, that society is present in and through people. The reason I have circled around this point and it in a variety of ways is that as John Seeley the sociologist puts it, "Something in Western thoughtways makes this line of thought extremely difficult. . . . Somehow, in Western thought, as in that of a small child, society is set outside come at it in a variety of ways is that as John Seeley the sociologist puts it, "Something in Western thoughtways makes this line of thought extremely difficult. . . . Somehow, in Western thought, as in that of a small child, society is set outside and over against the self, with some ridiculous and indefensible boundary drawn at the anatomical (and hence irelevant) skin" (Seeley, p. 114). Seeley may exaggerate the self, to talk of society oppressing all individuals. And one of the main themes of this book has been that this simple dichotomy between individual and society is not tenable in the light of present social-psychological knowledge.

Thus I wish to conceptualize both individual and society as made up of parts, and to see any given segment of society as encompassing only fragments of individuals. One of the implications of seeing individual and society as made up of parts is that just as conflict is made possible, so are coordination and cooperation, and here Schelling's ideas are pertinent. Schelling is interested in what he calls *tacit coordination;* and this ability to figure out what other people will do next and to coordinate one's own actions with theirs flows, just as inevitably as conflict does, from the fact that people are divided into parts, and are therefore capable of identifying part of themselves with another person. Thus communication can occur, and must occur if we are to build up the shared conceptualizations and symbolic networks that Burke emphasizes. But communication can never be total. We neither communicate totally what we are, nor do we completely understand what the other is and says. By the same token, according to this model, conflict need not be total.

This model also leads us away from discussing a good society, or toward relinquishing the attempt to envision a totally good society which is good in all of its parts for all parts of all individuals. This will be very difficult for us Americans; something about us inclines us toward the search for a perfect society. From the very beginning we have felt that we are "housed in a gigantic and beneficent natural environment" (Cowen, p. 24), and we have been trying to form a City of the West which will fulfill our most passionate longings. As Michael Cowen says in his study (*City of the West: Emerson, America and Urban Metaphor*) we Americans have long been interested in having the best of all possible worlds. His analysis is worth quoting at some length, since it ties together a number of themes:

> City of the West cannot, at its most literary level, be termed a specifically or exclusively American metaphor. Under such versions of Atlantis and Eldorado, it had often appeared in European literature as a conventional symbol of the lush, the golden, the exotic, the mysterious, the visionary—and, especially, the elusive object of any passionate longing, of any yearning of the romantic heart. . . . In the present study, City of the West will be used as the summary concept for this characteristic American desire for the best of all possi-

ble worlds. It will stand for the American's unwilling-
ness to admit that the polarities of his experience—
between nature and civilization, between economic
abundance and moral integrity, between individualistic desires and society's demands—were inevitable or
necessary (Cowen, pp. 27 and 31).

Cowen's analysis clearly fits in with my own: that the seeing
of society as oppressing the individual is connected with a
search for a society which would be fully the "elusive object
of any passionate longing, of any yearning of the romantic
heart."

A better way to think of society is in terms of one segment
of society being more or less good for one part or another of
some individuals. This is vastly more complicated, but
nonetheless vital. Thus I discussed the thoughts of
Schelling and Burke partially in an attempt to stress this
kind of thinking. For as they both emphasize the ways in
which goods come intermingled with bads, they help us see
that there will always be some human dissatisfaction. The
traffic light epitomizes this kind of dissatisfaction, however
trivially, when the light is red and we are in a hurry; but
eliminating this kind of dissatisfaction is not possible so
long as there are other individuals who are also in a hurry.

But another reason I discussed Schelling and Burke is to
make clear my belief that there are ideas outside of officially
constituted social-psychology which may be important for
helping social psychologists to work out viable theory.
Psychologists, if they are to broaden their conceptual
structures, their theories, are going to have to turn to
nonpsychologists. They have to emerge from the narrow
professionalism in which they are now caught, and develop
ways of talking with others who, although not professional
psychologists, have rich psychological insights. Novelists
and literary critics, sociologists and politicians, actors and
salesmen: there are many kinds of people who either have
psychological knowledge (actors, salesmen, novelists) or
who are concerned with thinking about psychological matters (philosophers, literary critics, historians, sociologists),

and they all are presently not consulted by psychologists. Intellectually and professionally, psychologists are too standoffish.

The point in considering Burke is not to argue that he is a great psychological thinker, but rather that people not formally labeled psychologists have interesting psychological insights. One can proceed in psychology not just by performing experiments, but by reading interesting writers and engaging in intellectual dialogue of a sort which has lost its respectability with the rise of behaviorism and the animosity against armchair speculation.

Despite the obscurity and difficulty of their writing, existential psychologists do take thoughtful writing seriously. They take Kierkegaard seriously. And Kierkegaard's writing on dread, or Stendahl's on love,[3] are as important for psychologists as Watson's concepts of behaviorism, or Freud's concepts of identification; and much more important than most of the small experiments which are done now. But recognition of this importance is not widespread. Why? There is a reluctance to engage in thoughtful encounter with writings by those who are labeled philosophers or novelists or literary critics; and this reluctance can only be a hindrance to the development of a true psychology about people and their behavior and experience.

Another underlying theme of this book is that people are necessary to each other; however inevitable the corrosion and corruption may be, we need each other for a variety of reasons. We need each other to cooperate and get necessary things accomplished. Babies need people taking care of them if they are to grow up, if they are to develop. Finally, as Goffman makes clear, grown-up people need one another to maintain a sense of purpose, to maintain definitions of reality, to maintain a sense of identity; we get support from one another just as inevitably as we get what Laing calls invalidation from one another. Both processes—support and invalidation—are interwoven and cannot be separated from one another.

3. I owe this example to Joseph de Rivera.

Perhaps in concluding I should list the major points I have made, both in this final chapter and throughout the book. The list.is somewhat artificial, since these ideas have not been separated in the text in just this way, but run together.

1. Conceptual analysis is important if social-psychological theory is to be developed. This means a respect for ideas, and more sustained attempts to analyze ideas; only if these become more characteristic of social psychology are we likely to develop a more comprehensive and satisfactory theory.

2. Social-psychological theory ought to bear upon social criticism, and part of our obligation as social psychologists is to show how our theories illuminate matters of general social importance and discussion.

3. Many important ideas—ways of putting things together, ways of seeing connections—may be available outside of officially constituted psychology. Thus psychologists ought, more regularly than they now do, to consult work by such nonpsychologists as literary critics, philosophers, historians, and especially novelists and playwrights.

4. Much of contemporary social criticism moves from an idea of what we call *radical autonomy*: the ideal which is being held up, in the light of which contemporary social reality is being criticized, is an idea which pictures an autonomous person, free of social constraint. This ideal of personal autonomy is oversimplified as it has been conventionally presented (although perhaps there is a way to work out a concept of autonomy which would also leave room for the points we have made about the necessary and inevitable constraints of sociability).

Social criticism today also seems to move from an overly simple conception of society as unitary in two ways: such criticism describes the present social *reality* as uniformly *bad*, and also describes the social *ideal* as uniformly *good*. None of this provides a guide for action; it is not the kind of thinking which helps us see more clearly what has to be done if we are to change society and/or the individual.

5. Society and the individual might better be conceived as made up of parts. Following this line of thought, our vision of the good society might give way to an analysis of how some segments of society are good or bad for some parts of some people at some particular time. This is vastly more complicated, but ultimately much more helpful.

6. Because people have different parts, they can get into partial conflict with one another (conflict need not be total); likewise, people can also cooperate with each other even while being in conflict with each other.

7. Because people and societies are made up of parts, they can change, although this is not to say that they necessarily will.

8. People become divided into parts either (a) because they are born that way, or (b) because they grow up in a situation where they are exposed to a variety of pressures from a variety of more powerful human beings, pressures which are internalized to some degree and resisted to some degree. This growing up process is terribly complex, and any juxtaposition of simple metaphors such as sculpturing or gardening does not begin to account for this process.

9. People are necessary to one another in a variety of ways: (a) to get things done (cooperation); (b) to become people (babies need help from others in order to grow up); and (c) to continue to be human (adults need ongoing support from one another, to maintain their identities, to maintain a feeling that life is worthwhile).

10. Much of this analysis is difficult for Americans to understand since there is something in us and our culture which leads us to conceive of the self as, ideally, imperial and autonomous and authentic in opposition to a corrupt society.

That concludes my listing of conclusions. If I have been successful, I have managed to tie these different themes together in a connected, perhaps even seamless, argument. No one or two of these points strikes me as being crucial; rather, they all seem to flow into one another. May the reader see that also!

Bibliography

Allport, Gordon. *Becoming*. New Haven: Yale University Press, 1955.

Aronson, Eliot. *The Social Animal*. San Francisco: W. H. Freeman and Company, 1972.

Back, Kurt. *Beyond Words*. New York: Russell Sage Foundation, 1972.

Becker, Ernest. *The Birth and Death of Meaning*. New York: The Free Press, 2d edition, 1971.

Berger, Peter. *Invitation to Sociology*. New York: Doubleday Anchor paperback, 1963.

Berman, Marshall. Book review of Erving Goffman, *Relations in Public*, *The New York Times Book Review*, February 27, 1972.

Berne, Eric. *Games People Play*. New York: Grove Press, 1964.

Bettelheim, Bruno. *Children of the Dream*. New York: Macmillan, 1969. Quotations from Avon paperback edition, 1970.

Breines, Paul. *Critical Interruptions*. New York: Herder and Herder, 1970.

Brown, Merle. *Kenneth Burke*. Minneapolis: University of Minnesota, 1969. (No. 75 in its series of pamphlets on American writers.)

Brown, Norman O. *Life Against Death*. New York: Random House, 1959.

———. *Love's Body.* New York: Random House, 1966.

Brown, Roger. *Social Psychology.* New York: Free Press, 1965.

Burke, Kenneth. *A Grammar of Motives.* New York: Prentice-Hall, 1945.

———. *A Rhetoric of Motives.* Cleveland: The World Publishing Company, 1962 (paperback edition).

———. *Attitudes Towards History* (rev. ed.). Boston: Beacon Press, 1961 paperback.

———. *Counter-Statement* (2d ed.) Los Altos, California: Hermes Publications, 1953.

———. *Language as Symbolic Action.* Berkeley, California: University of California Press, 1968.

———. *Permanence and Change* (2d rev. ed.). Los Altos, California: Hermes Publications, 1954.

———. *The Philosophy of Literary Form* (abridged). New York: Vintage Books, 1961.

Chein, Isidor. *The Science of Behavior and the Image of Man.* New York: Basic Books, 1972.

Cowen, Michael. *City of the West.* New Haven: Yale University Press, 1967.

Cruso, Thalassa. *Making Things Grow.* New York: Knopf, 1971.

Dahrendorf, Ralf. *Class and Class Conflict in Industrial Society.* Stanford, Calif: Stanford University Press, 1959.

Deutsch, Morton and Krauss, Richard. *Theories in Social Psychology.* New York: Basic Books, 1965.

Duncan, H. D. *Communication and Social Order.* New York: Bedminister Press, 1962.

———. *Language and Literature in Society.* Chicago: University of Chicago Press, 1953.

Ellman, Richard, ed. *The Artist as Critic: Critical Writings of Oscar Wilde.* New York: Vintage Books, 1970.

Erikson, Erik. *Childhood and Society.* New York: Norton, 1950 (2d ed., 1963).

Frank, Armin P. *Kenneth Burke.* New York: Twayne Publishers, 1969.

Frankl, Viktor. "Beyond Self-Actualization and Self-Expression," *Journal of Existential Psychiatry*, 1, 1960, pp. 5-20.

Freire, Paolo. *The Pedagogy of the Oppressed*. New York: Herder and Herder, 1970.

Freud, Sigmund. *A General Introduction to Psychoanalysis*. New York: Washington Square Press paperback, 1952.

———. *Civilization and Its Discontents*. In Vol. 21 of the *Standard Edition of the Complete Psychological Works of Sigmund Freud*. New York: Macmillan, 1964.

Friedenberg, Edgar. *Coming of Age in America*. New York: Random House, 1965.

Gagnon, John. "The Creation of the Sexual in Early Adolescence," in Kagan and Coles, *12 to 16: Early Adolescence*. New York: Norton, 1972, pp. 231-57.

Glass, John and Staude, John, eds. *Humanistic Society*. Pacific Palisades, Calif: Goodyear Publishing Company, 1972.

Goffman, Erving. *Asylums*. New York: Anchor paperback, 1961.

———. *Relations in Public*. New York: Harper Colophon paperback, 1972.

———. *The Presentation of Self in Everyday Life*. New York: Anchor paperback, 1959.

Hanson, Norwood. *Patterns of Discovery*. Cambridge, England: Cambridge University Press, 1965.

Harmon, Willis. "The New Copernican Revolution," in Theobald, ed. *Futures Conditional*. Indianapolis: Bobbs-Merrill, 1972, pp. 180-189.

Harris, Thomas. *I'm OK, You're OK*. New York: Harper and Row, 1969.

Henry, Jules. *On Sham and Vulnerability*. New York: Vintage Book, 1973.

———. *Pathways to Madness*. New York: Random House, 1971.

Holland, Virginia. *Counterpoint: Kenneth Burke and Aristotle's Theories of Rhetoric*. New York: The Philosophical Library, Inc. 1959.

Holt, John. "Letter," in *Commentary*, August, 1970, p. 6.

Hsu, Francis, ed. *Psychological Anthropology* (rev. ed.). Cambridge, Mass.: Schenkman Publishing Company, 1972.

Hunter, Edward. *Brainwashing in Red China*. New York: Vanguard Press, 1951.

Hyman, Stanley Edgar. *The Armed Vision* (rev. abridged ed.). New York: Vintage Books, 1955.

Jacoby, Russell. "Reversals and Lost Meanings," in Breines, ed. *Critical Interruptions*, New York: Herder and Herder, 1970, pp. 60-73.

Kagan, Jerome and Coles, Robert, eds. *12 to 16: Early Adolescence*. New York: Norton, 1972.

Kahn, Michael. "The Physiology of Catharsis," *Journal of Personality and Social Psychology*, 3 (1966), pp. 278-98.

Katz, Michael. *Class, Bureaucracy and Schools*. New York: Praeger, 1971.

Keniston, Kenneth. *The Uncommitted*. New York: Dell Publishing, 1970.

Kinkade, Kathleen. *A Walden Two Experiment*. New York: William Morrow, 1973.

Knox, George. *Critical Moments: Kenneth Burke's Categories and Critiques*. Seattle: University of Washington Press, 1957.

Laing, Ronald D. *Self and Others* (2d rev. ed.). New York: Pantheon Books, 1969. My page references are to the first edition, Chicago: Quadrangle books, 1962, unless otherwise noted.

———. *The Divided Self*. Baltimore: Pelican paperback, 1965.

———. "The Obvious," in Hendrik, Ruitenbeek, ed. *Going Crazy*. New York: Bantam Books, 1972. pp. 109-28.

———. *The Politics of Experience*. Baltimore: Penguin paperback, 1967.

———. *The Politics of the Family*. New York: Vintage Books, 1972.

——— and Esterson, Aaron. *Sanity, Madness and the Family*. Baltimore: Pelican paperback, 1970.

———, Phillipson, H. and Lee, A.R. *Interpersonal Perception.* New York: Perennial paperback, Harper and Row, 1972.

Lauter, Paul, and Howe, Florence. "How the School System is Rigged for Failure," *New York Review of Books,* 14, June 18, 1970, pp. 14-21.

Lidz, Theodore, Fleck, Stephen and Cornelison, Alice. *Schizophrenia and the Family.* New York: International Universities Press, 1965.

Luce, R.D. and Raiffa, R. *Games and Decisions.* New York: Wiley, 1957.

MacIntyre, Alasdair. *Herbert Marcuse.* New York: Viking Books, 1970.

Marcuse, Herbert. *An Essay on Liberation.* Boston: Beacon, 1969.

———. *Eros and Civilization.* Boston: Beacon, 1955.

———. "Love Mystified," in *Negations.* Boston: Beacon paperback, 1969. This essay was first published in *Commentary,* February, 1967.

———. *One-Dimensional Man.* Boston: Beacon paperback, 1966.

———. "Repressive Tolerance," in Wolff, Robert Paul, Moore, Barrington and Marcuse, Herbert. *A Critique of Pure Tolerance.* Boston: Beacon paperback, 1969.

———. "The Obsolescence of the Freudian Concept of Man," in *Five Lectures.* Boston: Beacon, 1970, pp. 44-61.

Maslow, Abraham. *Towards a Psychology of Being* (2d ed.). New York: Van Nostrand Reinhold, 1968.

May, Rollo, Angel, E. and Ellenberger, H., eds. *Existence.* New York: Basic Books, 1955.

Mills, C. Wright. *White Collar.* New York: Oxford University Press, 1951.

Mishler, Elliot. "Man, Morality and Madness: Critical Perspectives on the Work of R.D. Laing," in Rubinstein, Benjamin, ed. *Psychoanalysis and Contemporary Science.* New York: Macmillan, 1973, Volume II, pp. 369-93.

Poirier, Richard. *A World Elsewhere.* New York: Oxford University Press paperback, 1968.

Polanyi, Michael. *Personal Knowledge*. London: Routledge and Kegan Paul, 1958.

Reich, Charles A. *The Greening of America*. New York: Random House, 1970.

Rogers, Carl. "A Humanistic Conception of Man," in Glass and Staude, *Humanistic Society*. Pacific Palisades, Calif.: Goodyear Publishing Company, 1972.

———. *Becoming Partners*. New York: Dell, 1972.

———. *Client-Centered Therapy*. Boston: Houghton-Mifflin, 1951.

———. "Interpersonal Relationships: USA 2000," *Journal of Applied Behavioral Science*, 4, 1968, pp. 265-80.

———. *On Becoming a Person*. Boston: Houghton-Mifflin, 1961.

———. *On Encounter Groups*. New York: Harper and Row, 1970.

———. *Person to Person*. Lafayette, California: Real People Press, 1967.

Rosenthal, Robert. *Experimenter Effects in Behavioral Research*. New York: Appleton-Century Crofts, 1966.

Roszak, Theodore. *The Making of a Counter-Culture*. Garden City, New York: Doubleday, 1969.

Rueckert, William, ed. *Critical Responses to Kenneth Burke, 1924-1966*. Minneapolis, Minn.: University of Minnesota, 1969.

———. *Kenneth Burke and the Drama of Human Relations*. Minneapolis, Minn.: University of Minnesota, 1963.

Schein, Edgar H. *Coercive Persuasion*. Cambridge, Mass.: Massachusetts Institute of Technology, 1961.

Schelling, Thomas. "On the Ecology of Micromotives," *Public Interest*, 1971, # 25, pp. 59-98.

———. *The Strategy of Conflict*. Cambridge, Mass.: Harvard University Press, 1960.

Seeley, John. *The Americanization of the Unconscious*. New York: J. Aronson, 1967.

Slater, Philip. *Earthwalk*. New York: Doubleday, 1974.

———. *Microcosm: Structural, Psychological, and Religious Evolution in Groups*. New York: Wiley, 1966.

———. *The Pursuit of Loneliness*. Boston: Beacon Press, 1970.

Skinner, B.F. *Walden Two*. New York: Macmillan paperback, 1962.

Sypher, Wylie. *Loss of the Self in Modern Literature and Art*. New York: Random House, 1962.

Theobald, Robert, ed. *Futures Conditional*. Indianapolis: Bobbs-Merrill, 1972.

Trilling, Lionel. *Beyond Culture*. New York: Viking, 1965.

———. *Matthew Arnold* (rev. ed.). New York: Columbia University Press, 1949. Quotations from Meridian paperback edition, 1953.

———. *Sincerity and Authenticity*. Cambridge, Mass.: Harvard University Press, 1972.

von Neumann, J. and Morgenstern, Oscar. *Theory of Games and Economic Behavior*. Princeton: Princeton University Press, 1944.

Weber, Shierry. "Individuation as Praxis," in Breines, Paul, ed. *Critical Interruptions*. New York: Herder and Herder, 1972, pp. 22-59.

Zinsser, Hans. *Rats, Lice and History*. New York: Bantam Books, 1971.

INDEX

Certain issues are discussed throughout the book and are thus not listed separately in the index: the self and its unity or lack of it (fragmentation); society's impact on the self: is it helpful, or harmful? does its pressures help increase unity or rather promote fragmentation?; society and its structure and organization: is it unified or fragmented?; communication and its effects on people; conflict (within people and in society); the importance of theory in psychology; conceptual problems which exist in various theoretical orientations; psychology and its contribution to understanding people and society.